Whole Business Architecture

Exploring the context of Business Architecture

Tom Graves

JC3DVIS
CONCEPT DESIGN

Published by
JC3DVIS

www.jc3dvis.co.uk

First published July 2024
ISBN 9781739125486 (Paperback)
First Edition

Legal disclaimer

CGI illustrations, design and editing by JC3DVIS

Whole Business Architecture

Exploring the context of Business Architecture

Tom Graves

Contents

Part 1: Business-Architecture

Part 2: Business-architecture challenges

Part 3: Business-generalist

Part 4: Business-futures

What is *Whole Business Architecture?*

'Business'-architecture is often defined as a subset of 'enterprise'-architecture, which itself is misdefined as a subset of IT-governance. This book looks at how business-architecture fits into the wider context of an enterprise.

In this book an **business** is defined as:
The main activity of an organisation, such as providing a service or product, while making a profit.

And **architecture** is defined as:
The structure and story of how everything works together as a whole.
In an airport, for example, a building architect would tackle the physical aspects of the building, the air-conditioning, doors etc. A solution architect would typically tackle the IT aspects of the airport, such as the software needed to run the airport, assisting: visas, luggage, information flow and much more, while an business architect would tackle all of the parts of the business, connecting the boxes.

So **Whole business architecture** is defined as:
The architecture of 'the business of the business', and how it connects with all the other architectures aided by enterprise-architecture, whose role is to ensure that all the different architectures work well together.

This book is a collection of edited articles which pose important questions about business-architecture. In addition, illustrations help explain key concepts to help you better architect your business.

This book acts as a bridge to a huge library of work produced over thirty years in the field of business architecture and as a companion to the book: **Whole Enterprise Architecture**.

Most of the chapters reference more 'in-depth' articles which can be found in a set of anthologies at **www.leanpub.com/u/tetradian** .

Tom Graves has been an independent consultant for more than four decades, in business transformation, enterprise architecture and knowledge management. His clients in Europe, Australasia and the Americas cover a broad range of industries including small-business, banking, utilities, manufacturing, logistics, engineering, media, telecoms, research, defence and government. He has a special interest in whole-enterprise architectures for non-profit, social, government and commercial enterprises.

Part 1:

Business-architecture

This section of the book is an abridged version of
Business architecture basics'
www.leanpub.com/tp-bizarch

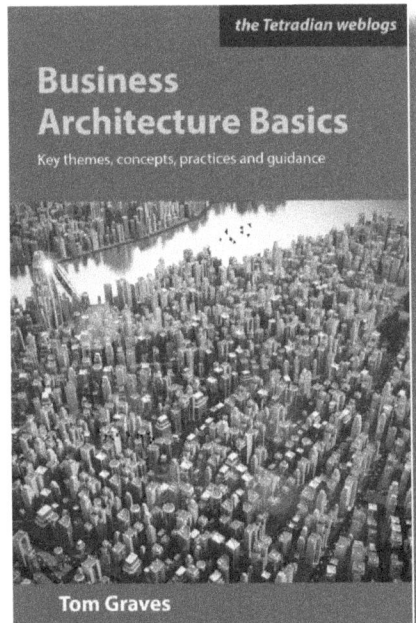

1: What do we mean by 'business-architecture'?

One of the keys to breaking free from IT-focused *'enterprise'*-architecture lies in reclaiming the meaning of the term *'business-architecture'.*

In *'classic'* enterprise-architecture, everything revolves around IT: the IT is seen as the centre of meaning within the enterprise.
'Business'-architecture is defined as a subset of *'enterprise'*-architecture, which itself is defined as a subset of IT-governance. And in practice, business-architecture is viewed as a near-random grab-bag of *'anything not-IT that might affect IT'*, without any real clarity about how that grab-bag is structured within itself, and with no acknowledgement at all about anything that might not affect IT. Certainly not something that we could use at an enterprise level.

So the first step outward is to start to treat business-architecture as a form of architecture in its own right. That's starting to happen now. People are at last beginning to break free from the trap of focusing solely on IT.

Yet there's another trap that comes right after that one, that a lot of people are falling straight into it: Business-centrism. Where *'the business'* is seen as the centre of the architecture, around which everything else revolves.
In a true enterprise-architecture, everywhere and nowhere is the centre. It has to be that way: otherwise it is **not** an enterprise-architecture.

Which means that, to quote the late *Len Fehskens*, "Business-architecture is *merely a domain-architecture, one of many other domain architectures, just like IT-architecture is a domain-architecture (or a cluster of related domain-architectures, rather)*". It is a subset of *'the architecture of the enterprise'*, with responsibility for an explicit domain of interrelated concerns within that overall scope.

To me it is literally ***the architecture of the business***, in other words, *'the business of the business',* how its core business is organised and structured, usually at a fairly abstract level. *Like most domain-architectures, it typically focusses at Zachman level-3, 'Logical'*[1].

Given that description of boundaries, a core part of that structure represented by and maintained in the business-architecture is the business-model *(or set of business-models)*. In the *Osterwalder* sense, which is the one I use here, though in perhaps a more extended sense than in *Osterwalder's Business Model Canvas*. A *'business-model'* is a structure, one that provides the central focus for *'the business of the business'.*

---

1. Zachman levels
See Whole EA, page 36, for more information about Zachman levels.

It is not much about vision or values, or strategy, those are inputs to the business-architecture.
It is not much about the details of business-process: that is the role of process-architecture *(these days often known as BPM, Business Process Management)*, or IT-architecture, or often both in parallel.

It is not about the physical structures in which those processes take place: that is the role of facilities architecture, or the literal architecture of buildings. It is not about the skill-sets or organisational structures to operate or manage those processes: that is the role of HR and organisational-architecture. And so on.

Business-architecture **is** about the architecture of *'the business of the business',* and how it connects with all the other architectures aided by enterprise-architecture, whose role is to ensure that all the different architectures work well together.

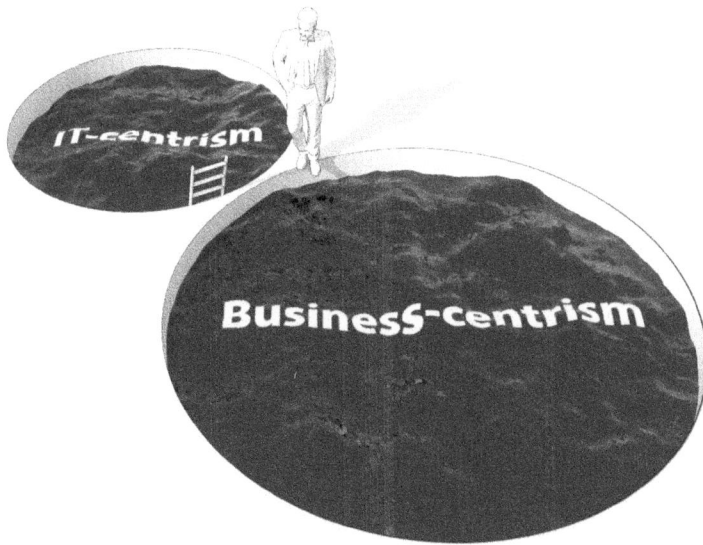

People are breaking free from the trap of focusing solely on IT, yet there's another trap that comes right after that, Business-centrism.

2: Business-architect and Enterprise-architect

Enterprise business-architecture is an important aspect of enterprise-architectures; done properly, it is not an IT-role. But at present it is still all too often portrayed as such; and the relationships between the various roles have become blurred and confused. To the point where that confusion is causing a lot of damage to organisations and their business-related architectures, and to the profession as a whole.

The core of the problem is two issues:
- *portraying enterprise-architecture as a minor subset of IT-governance*
- *portraying business-architecture as a kind of random grab-bag of 'anything not-IT' that might affect IT*

Many are aware of these issues including, the late *Len Fehskens*, who had been fighting this particular battle for even longer than I have.

His description of roles is really useful here: *xA*, *ExA*, *EA* *(about which more in a moment)*. In essence, the architect's role consists of bringing things together into some kind of unified whole, for a chosen purpose.

The key point is that to understand and describe the role, we need to understand both its scope *(or 'width')* and its direct skill-level *(or 'depth')*.

A domain is a region of scope and expertise: for example, IT-infrastructure, security, brand, organisation, process, logistics and so on. In *Len's* description, '*x*' is any specific domain:

- **xA** *(e.g. an applications-architect or brand-architect).*
  A domain architect, with emphasis on a single domain or closely-related cluster of domains, almost always with high skill-level (strong depth) in that domain.
- **ExA** *(e.g. EBA, 'enterprise business-architect'; EITA, 'enterprise IT-architect').*
  An enterprise-scope domain-architect, with emphasis on how a single domain links with other domains; the skill-level is sometimes referred as 'T-shaped', deep-skill in one domain, but sufficient knowledge of other domains to be able to support good ability to converse with other domain-architects and other specialists from those other domains.
- **EA**: *An enterprise architect is a specific domain-architect whose domain is the enterprise as a whole, and for whom the core skill-set includes cross-context specialisms such as systems-theory, human-factors, futures, strategy and other 'big-picture' themes; the skill-level across domains tends to be broad rather than deep ('comb-shaped' rather than 'T-shaped'), but must include all domains that are in scope for the enterprise.*

In most countries, by law, the only people who can describe themselves as 'architects', without any other qualifier, are building-architects. Everyone else in all other cross-context linking or cross-domain-linking professions must use some kind of qualifier, for example: naval-architects, civil-architects, security-architects and, of course, enterprise-architects.

What some have done is to completely scramble that description: routinely, an IT domain-architecture or, at best, an **EITA**[1] is labelled as an *'EA'*, with business-architecture. What should be a domain that is business-focussed and functionally distinct from IT, is parked randomly *'under'* the IT-focused *'EA'* banner. Meaning that *'business-architecture'* is simultaneously both *'below'* and *'above'* that *'enterprise-architecture'*, making an unusable mess.

Unfortunately it may well be true that *'business'* architect is currently described as an IT role. But it really doesn't help to do so. Every one of us needs to be clear about this, because it is probably the primary cause of damage to the profession at present.

Business-architecture is a distinct domain, the architecture of *'the business of the business',* that must not be seen as *'above'* the scope of the broader shared enterprise in which the business operates. By definition, it's *'under'* EA, because EA provides the overall umbrella under which everything connects with everything else. But when only IT-architectures are described as *'EA'*, then there are some circumstances in which BA or EBA is *'above'* that kind of *'EA'*. Yet also circumstances when they're not, given the way that some describe BA and EA. Which again adds to the mess…

Which is where we come to the second issue : *Defining 'business-architecture' as 'anything not-IT that might affect IT'.* No wonder that business-people get seriously annoyed at IT-centric *'EA'* and its description of *'business'*-architecture that makes no business sense.

So we have many in the *'enterprise-architecture'* space, describing an *'enterprise architecture'* that isn't about the enterprise as enterprise, and a *'business-architecture'* that has very little connection with the business of the business.
It may be *'realism'* to say that *"Business Architect, nowadays, sadly, is an IT job"*, but it is not wise to allow that misnaming to go unchallenged, because the consequences are very serious indeed.

---

1. EITA
Enterprise Information Technology Architecture

⬠⬠⬠⬠⬠ *Taken from the chapter:* **Business architect and enterprise architect**

3: Business-architect or Enterprise-architect, part 2

I do not have any problem with the term *'Enterprise Business Architect'*, I think it is an entirely valid description of an architectural role. Let me explain.

There is a role called *'architect'*. Someone whose job it is to link various things together in a consistent, integrated, maintainable and sustainable way. It could be any area at all, any focus or interest: as long as it's linking more than a couple of different types of items together, you could just about get away with calling the role an *'architect'*.

Often we will find there's a prefix, specifying a technology, or a domain of interest, or something like that. In more detail we will see titles like *Siebel architect* or *web architect*. Going up a level or two, we will see more emphasis on the domain: *process-architect*, *security-architect*, and so on.

Each of these roles has a strong specialist element, emphasising the particular domain of interest, and usually a lot of in-depth knowledge and skills in that specialism. But they're more than just specialists. They are what we might call *'T-shaped'*: a lot of depth in one domain, but also a bit of depth in a range of other domains too. Which is what gives them the ability to make links between domains, and makes them *'architects'*.

Architects have a lot of depth in one domain, and a bit of depth in others.

And each of these domain-architectures requires its own distinct skill-sets, each with their own distinct terminologies and concerns. And the depth required is such that they are often incompatible with each other, too. But an *'architect'* is someone who can link across those incompatibilities. Then we will sometimes find that there is a need for a scope-prefix on the name, of which the most common is the term *'enterprise'*, meaning that the work has an enterprise-wide scope. This scope-prefix, if present, should always come before the domain-prefix. For example *'Enterprise Siebel-architect'* compared to *'Siebel enterprise architect'*.

The point is that there's a special-case, where it's not that the domain has a specific scope, but that the scope itself *is* the domain.

To use a term coined by *David Armano*, we could describe these architects as *'sun-shaped'.* They are true generalists, linking across every sub-domain within that scope. And that's a distinct skill-set in itself, radically different from the domain-specific skills of the *'T-shaped'* domain-architects. The only person who should be called an *'enterprise architect'* is one whose domain is the entire scope of the enterprise.

To me a business-architect is a domain-specialist: someone who specialises in the architecture of *'the business of the business'.*

These are typically people who've expanded outward from business-analysis. By which I mean *'the analysis of business'*, in-depth financials and so on, not the IT-oriented notion of *"someone who gets IT requirements from 'the business'"*. They have learnt enough of other domains to act as architects, but their real focus will be in *'business'*-type themes such as business-models, investment-planning, financial modelling and so on.

These business-architects are specialists, with distinct business-oriented specialist skills. A business-architect will typically work within one business-unit, or perhaps a whole company within a conglomerate.

An enterprise business-architect is one who would cover the whole portfolio of the business-as-enterprise. But it is still business-architecture, *'the architecture of business'*, it doesn't move much outside of that domain. For example, it would not usually cover IT-implementation, or detail-level process-design, and so, it's about *'the business of business'*, and not much more.

But an enterprise-architect covers the entire scope: every domain, at every level. The role also covers a scope that can extend much further out than that of the business-architect. An enterprise-architect must be able to separate the organisation and enterprise where required. Extending the enterprise-in-scope beyond the legal-responsibility boundaries that define the organisation, to encompass:
• *the supply-chain*
• *the market*
• *the direct business-ecosystem*
• *the community*
• *government and sometimes even further than that.*

The time-scales may also be much longer than those of the business-architect: the latter may well be concerned with a five-year strategy at most, whereas environmental and other concerns mean that the enterprise-architect may at times need to consider an indefinite or even infinite timescale.

An enterprise-architect must also be comfortable working at any level, from the board-room to the factory-floor, from operations to tactics to strategy and beyond; and with concerns that may be deep within and/or far beyond the organisation itself. This demands a skill-set that is broad rather than deep, focussed on interconnections more than on item-detail, an unusual ability to learn the basics of any skill or domain very quickly indeed. This is a very different skill-set from that of the *'business-oriented'* business-architect. I don't think I have ever met anyone who truly managed to combine both sets of skills in their personal portfolio, and I don't think it's fair to expect anyone to do so, especially across all of the complexities of a typical large organisation.

What worries me somewhat is that the role of business-architect is likely to become confused with that of the true enterprise-architect. We used to see a lot of IT-architects who called themselves *'enterprise-architects',* yet who really were not aware about anything that happened outside of IT. Which could lead to problems as soon as they tried to tackle a true enterprise-architecture scope.

A domain architecture is centred on that domain *(and arguably should be, too)*; but an enterprise-architecture has to cover everything, as exact equals, everywhere. That is what makes it different. That is also what makes it hard to do.

So yes, there is a real role called the Enterprise Business Architect. It can be done by the same person who does the role of Enterprise Architect; but in practice it's usually not a good idea to try to do that, because the skill-sets that the roles require are so different from each other.

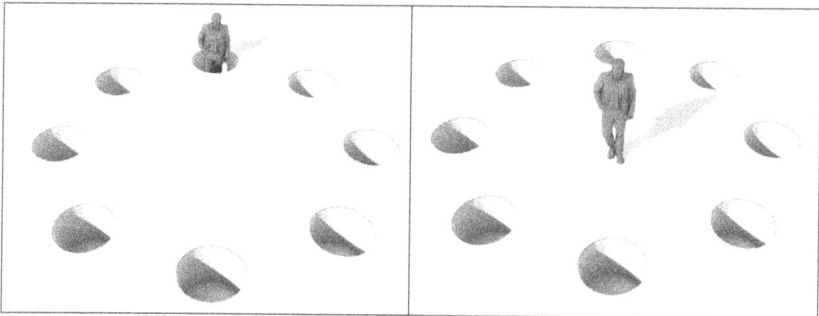

*Domain Architecture (left) is focused on a specific domain, while EA (right) looks in less detail at **all** domains of an enterprise.*

4: More about business-architecture and EA

There are some very real dangers in business-centrism. Jumping from IT-centrism to business-centrism has many potential problems.

To get round that mistake, we need always to remember that in a viable architecture, everywhere and nowhere is *'the centre of the architecture'*, all at the same time.

Yet the real reason why this matters to everyone goes a little bit deeper.

The real reason is **stakeholders**.

Who they are.
What they want.
What they will do.
What they will do to us, if we mess things up. *(As they perceive it, not us.)*

In which case, how do you identify your stakeholders?

If we are working at a solution-architecture level, this might not sound like a big deal. Who are your stakeholders? There is the project-sponsor. A consultant or two, perhaps. A few middle-managers somewhere, maybe even someone on the executive board. But that would be about it, usually. But as we move outward towards an enterprise-architecture level, holding onto the same assumptions about stakeholders will lead to problems. That is because the real definition of *'stakeholder'* is anyone who can wield a sharp-pointed stake in our direction. And if we ever forget that, or if we ever forget just how many stakeholders we really have, then we are asking for trouble. Let's describe this visually. At the start, we might we sit in the comforting self-centred view that the only stakeholders that matter are those inside our own organisation, shown below:

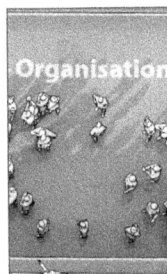

Part of the Whole EA tool looking at internal stakeholders.
Original version designed by Tom Graves and Michael Smith.

But when we start looking at our transactions, we can see that suppliers and customers are stakeholders as well.

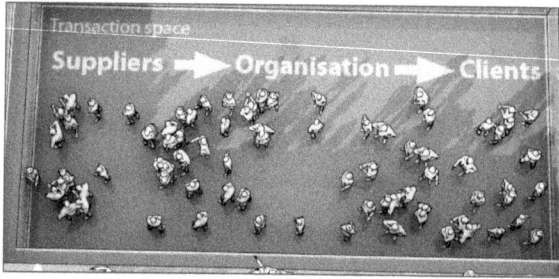

Looking beyond internal stakeholders

And what about competitors, regulators, journalists, trainers and others like that? We don't have transactions with them, but we have interactions with them that can matter a lot.

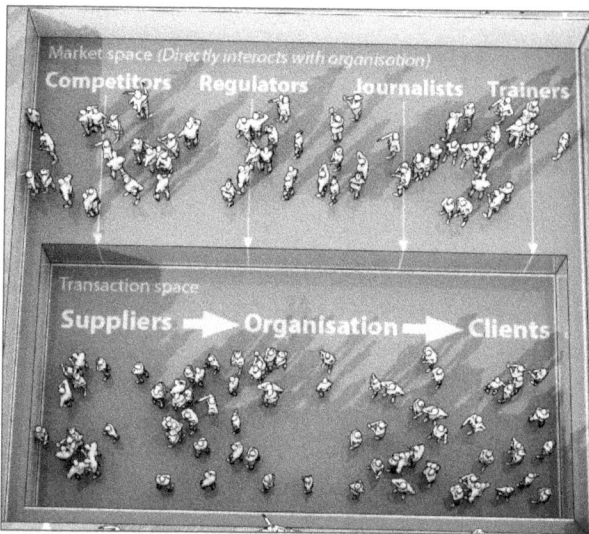

A wider group of stakeholders

If we think enterprise-architecture is just *'business-architecture plus IT'*, that is probably where we would stop. But that would be a mistake, because we need to go a whole lot further…

For a start, there's the shareholders, the *'owners'*.

They connect in a more indirect way, through a different set of channels, but we must not forget about them as stakeholders.

If we recognise that there is a lot more to business than just the money, we can then see that shareholders and such like are just one special case amongst a whole myriad of other forms of investment in the enterprise as a whole, as a shared-story.

That is when we start a more systematic exploration of our business context, and begin to grasp just how many types of stakeholders we really have:

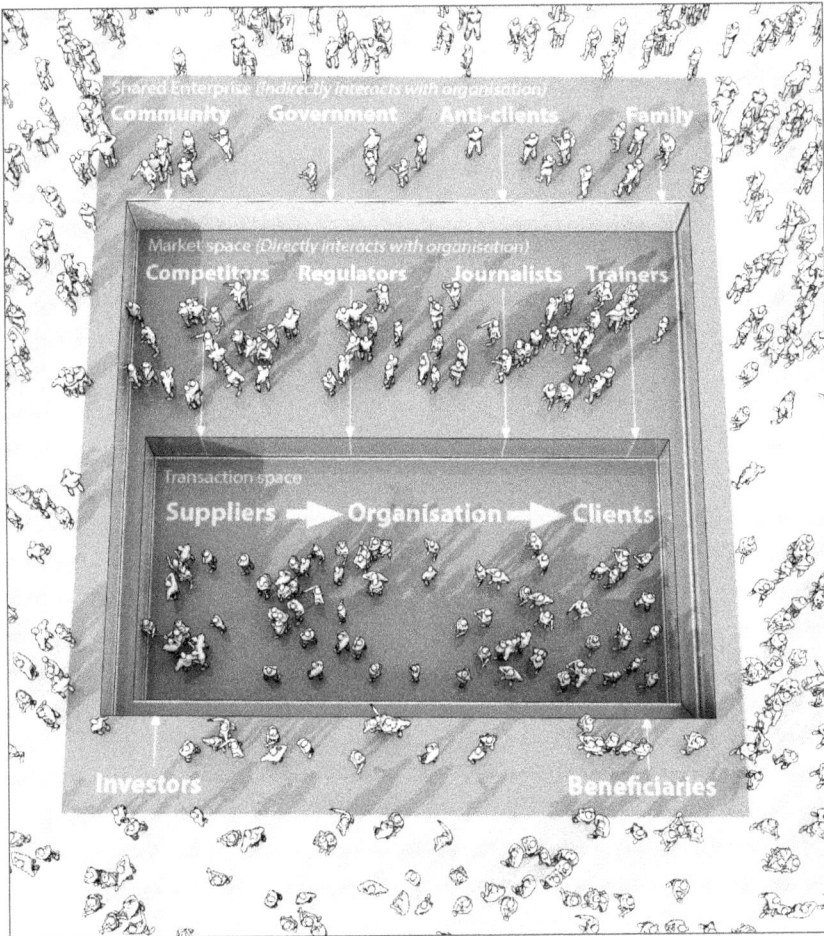

We can begin to grasp just how many types of stakeholders we really have.

Taken from the chapter: **On business-architecture and enterprise-architecture - why this matters**

5: Business-architecture frameworks

What is Business Architecture? What does a Business Architecture Framework look like?

Business-architecture proper is the strategy layer. *Zachman Framework (see overleaf) row-2 and upward, also bridging down into row-3.*
Instead, think of the remainder of what some *'heavyweight frameworks'* call *'business architecture'* as two distinct layers:
• *the logical or integration layer, Zachman row-3 to row-4*
• *the physical or implementation layer, Zachman row-4 to row-5*

Zachman's structure of layers still works well for this. The only essential change is an extra *'row-zero'* for compatibility with the *Vision* layer of *ISO-9000:2000.* But it does need some rework on the columns.
For example, there is a dimension missing, to handle distinctions between physical assets *(things)*, virtual assets *(data etc)*, relational *(what your CRM is all about)*, aspirational assets *(morale and the like)*, and abstract *(such as the financials that business people want in their models).*
The same for locations *(physical, virtual, relational etc)* and so on.

Zachman makes the the key distinction between primitives and composites. As *Zachman* says, architecture is about primitives, whilst solutions come from composites or patterns. The *Zachman Framework* is a classification of primitives: root-level entities, some of them fairly abstract. Composites are structured collections of primitives that straddle the columns, making up patterns for re-use.

Composites are usable to the extent that they are architecturally *'complete'*, straddling all of the columns, but are re-usable to the extent that they are incomplete. For example, a BPMN[1] process-model says nothing about *'Where'* or *'Why'*, so can be re-used in different locations and *(in principle)* for different purposes. At the mid-layer of the framework, you need to be able to describe a process in abstract terms, to identify KPIs[2] and CSFs[3] and so on. You would define different SLAs[4] as you go down towards different implementations, manual, machine, IT, etc, but they should all use the same KPIs etc. This is important because if you are not able to anchor the detail-layer composites into their component sub-composites, all the way down to their root-primitives, you will not be able to see options for redesign, such as for disaster-recovery or process-reengineering.

---

1. BPMN (Business Process Model and Notation)
A graphic representation of an organisation's business processes.
2. KPI (Key Performance Indicator)
Used to measure the performance of a department, etc within an organisation.
3. CSF (Critical Success Factor)
An element which is needed in order for a project to succeed.
4. SLA (Service Level Agreement)
An agreement for the level of service offered, including how it is measured.

Think of the IT-focused assumption that every problem must always have an IT-based solution… your only way to avoid that trap is to use a non-IT focused framework that covers the true whole-of-enterprise space.

Over the past few years I have done quite a bit of work on a *'service oriented enterprise'* framework, based on the classic *Stafford Beer 'Viable System Model'.*[1]

We extended this at Australia Post and elsewhere to include support for quality-systems, security-management and so on.

A simplified version of the Zachman framework, which can be used to explore an enterprise at various levels of detail. For example, at the enterprise level for an airport we might have a broad overview. While at the operations/action-plan level we might have specific model numbers and timings.

1. Viable System Model
The viable system model (VSM) is a model of the organisational structure of any autonomous system capable of producing itself. Wikipedia

⬠⬠⬠⬠⬠ *Taken from the chapter: **Business-architecture frameworks***

6: Business-architecture governance

For all architecture, including architecture governance, I use an iterative, recursive[1] process that draws from the old Group Dynamics 5-step cycle:

1: Purpose ('Forming')

• What is the business purpose? Vision, values, mission, goals, objectives?
• Who does it serve?
• In what way will it serve?
• Recursively, what is the purpose of the business-architecture within this purpose?

Sources include internal visioning, futures techniques such as CLA[2], business-intelligence, market-intelligence and whole-of-enterprise architecture.

2. People ('Storming')

• Who are the stakeholders both within and beyond the business?
• Recursively, who are the stakeholders in the architecture?
• What is important to them, What are their concerns and values?
• What needs to be done to ensure communication, negotiation and engagement?

Sources include VPEC-T[3] assessment, market-intelligence, HR reviews and social-network analysis.

3. Preparation ('Norming')

• What processes exist for business-architecture development?
• Recursively, what processes exist for governance of business-architecture?
• How do these processes ensure alignment with purpose and engagement with stakeholders?

Sources include governance frameworks for architecture and governance within the business itself.

4. Practice ('Performing')

• Action the governance processes, recursively, as appropriate. Ensure alignment with purpose, engagement with stakeholders, conformance to process and (as per next step) gathering of the appropriate metrics.

---

1. Recursion
Recursion occurs when the definition of a concept or process depends on a simpler or previous version of itself. Wikipedia

2.CLA (Causal Layered Analysis)
CLA is a theory and method that seeks to integrate various learning modes of research. Wikipedia

VPEC-T (Value, Policies, Events, Content and Trust)
VPEC-T is a framework which provides a simplified language for preventing loss in translation from business needs to IT solutions. Wikipedia

5. Performance ('Mourning'/'Adjourning')

- *What metrics and qualitative evaluations are required to assess the results of the work in terms of the Purpose, People, Preparation and Practice?*
- *What reviews are needed to support the Purpose assessment in the next iteration of the overall cycle?*
- *Recursively, what metrics, evaluations and reviews are needed for the architecture itself, and of and for its governance?*

Many of the key metrics will be industry and enterprise specific.
Common examples of generic metrics include standard accounting-practice, sustainability metrics such as GRI[1] and Balanced Scorecard[2].
Internal benefits-realisation processes and lessons-learned assessments such as After Action Reviews will also be of value here.
The overall process is cyclic, the end of **step 5** should lead directly to **step 1** of a new iteration.

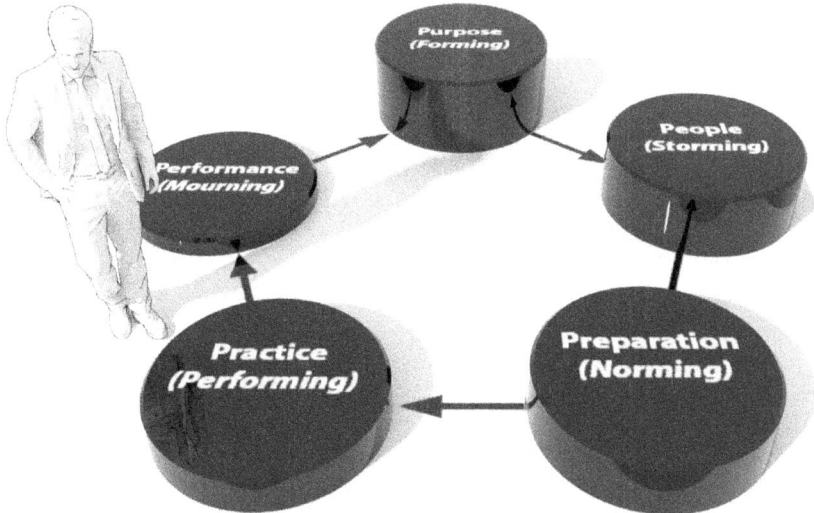

A simple version of the Group Dynamics 5-step cycle.

---

1. GRI (Global Reporting Initiative)
The GRI is an international independent standards organisation that helps businesses, governments, and other organisations understand and communicate their impacts on issues such as climate change, human rights, and corruption. Wikipedia

2. Balanced Scorecard
A balanced scorecard is a strategy performance management tool, a report used to keep track of the execution of activities by staff and to monitor the consequences arising from these actions. Wikipedia

---

⬠⬠⬠⬠⬠ *Taken from the chapter: **Business-architecture governance***

7: **The business of the business**

What is business? For that matter, what is, or is not, *'a business'*?

The usual answers I hear seem to revolve around an assumption that an organisation can only be called *'a business'* if its focus is *'making money'*, in other words some sort of *commercial* business.
Yet in which case, what do we call other types of organisations?
'Non-businesses', perhaps? If so, why does almost every government organisation, or charity, have people whose job-title is some variant of *'business-manager'*? And if only commercial organisations can be called *'businesses'*, what do we call the equivalent of business-architecture in those many organisations that, according that definition, are not *'businesses'*?

What I would suggest, is that this separation of *'business'* versus *'non-business'* is as artificial as the separation between *'for profit'* and *'not-for-profit'*, and just as misleading, too.

The simple way out of this one is to recognise that *'business'* literally means *'busy-ness'*, the state or condition of *'being busy'*. In which case, every organisation must, by definition, be *'a business'*, because the whole point of an organisation is that it provides a context to coordinate people's *'busy-ness'* towards a shared aim. Every organisation has its business; every organisation is *'a business'*.

In every organisation, the business of the business is whatever the business of that organisation happens to be, whether it's focussed on monetary profit, or not. If it's about *'busyness'*, it's business.

Which means, in turn, that every organisation has its own business-architecture, whatever type of organisation it may be.

Business-architecture is the architecture of the business of the business, whatever that organisation and its business might be.

More practically, the part of the organisation that's usually called *'the business'* tends to focus more on the why and how of the business. Rather than the who and when and where and with-what that tends to be more the focus of everyday operations. It tends to be about things like business-models, business-strategy, financials, forecasts, performance, monitoring, all the bigger-picture stuff. This is where business-architecture would usually place most of its attention.

And so, for practical reasons, typically because of the need for specific skills and suchlike, business-architecture will tend to be a domain-architecture focussed on that specific subsection of the organisation's activity, rather than the unifying architecture of the organisation as a whole.

Which is why there usually needs to be a distinction between business-architecture, the architecture of the business of the business, and enterprise-architecture. The unifying architecture of the overall organisation and its relationship with its broader business-context, linking all of the architecture-domains together. There's also the distinction that business architecture tends to look inside-in or inside-out, whereas a true *'architecture of the enterprise'* also needs to look outside-in and even outside-out.

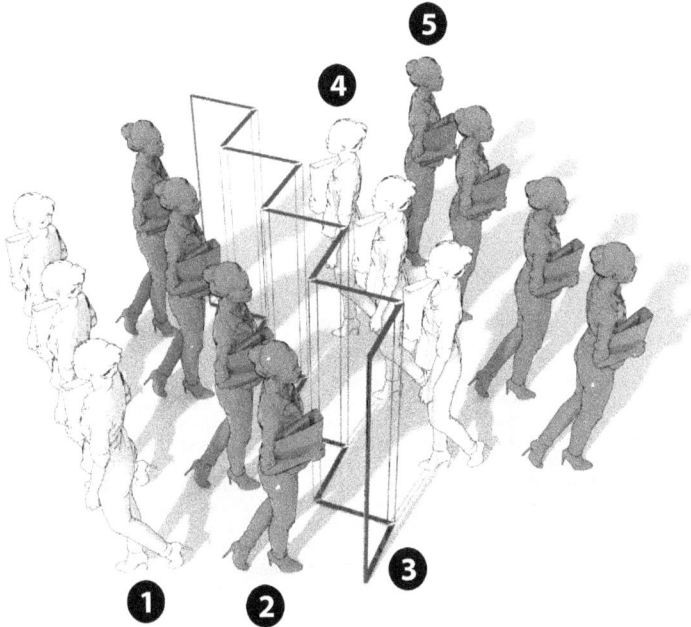

Four types of perspectives of an enterprise:

1 Inside-in
The world is viewed as if the organisation is the only thing that exists. .

2 Inside-out
The world is viewed as though it exists to serve the needs of the organisation.

3 Interaction journey
The interaction between the organisation and the client/customer.

4 Outside-in
The organisation is viewed as if it may be something that the world needs.

5 Outside-out
Is the *'world'* in its own terms, whether or not the organisation exists.

8: A checklist for business transformations

What is a key tool to help manage something as wide-ranging and complex as a business-transformation? Answer: a checklist.

The following checklist for business-transformations is adapted from one that we use in our own work on transformation.

1. Story and purpose

Do we have clarity about what the aims are for this transformation, and how do we describe those aims? What is the story here?
Use visioning and values-mapping to obtain a shared-story that links all potential players in the shared-enterprise.

2. Scope and stakeholders

Do we have clarity on scope and stakeholders for this transformation?
Map this out both within the organisation, and to at least three layers beyond it: transactions with suppliers and customers; direct interactions with other players in the broader market; and indirect interactions in the shared-enterprise space, such as government, communities, investors and anticlients. Connect this with the previous check to build appropriate value-governance for the context.

3. Context, scale and scaling

Do we have clarity on the applicable scale for this transformation, and how we manage increasing and/or decreasing scale?
Design tests for extremes from very-small to very-large, for example, Agile-type methods may work well for prototypes, but not for large-scale high-reliability operations.

4. Full-cycle governance

Do we have clarity on how we will guide not just initial change for the transformation, but for the entire life-cycle of everything arising from or affected by it?
This includes commissioning and decommissioning, development and maintenance of required knowledge and skill-sets, and anything else needed to guide and govern change throughout the entire life-cycle of everything arising from the transformation.

5. Structural flaws in the context

Do we have clarity on structural-flaws in the context for this transformation, that will need to be resolved for ongoing viability?
Note that larger-scope structural-flaws such as whole-of-context feedback-loops may only become visible when systems interact with each other across the whole shared-enterprise. Beware too of Conway's Law, that organisations tend to design systems that reflect the existing communication-structures of that organisation. We need to take care not to replicate existing structural-flaws into new system-designs.

6. Limits and constraints

Do we have clarity on all constraints that may apply within the context of the transformation?

This applies especially to non-negotiable constraints, such as those that arise from physics or from limits to scaling. For example, the speed of light becomes a very real constraint on options to reduce system-wide latency in high-speed communications at global scale.

7. Resistance to change

Do we have clarity on any resistance to change for this transformation, on the underlying drivers behind that resistance to change, and how to resolve those factors within the transformation?

For useful guidance on this, see standard references on the human side of change-management, such as Sengé et al's The Dance of Change.
For example, one key concern addressed in that book is how to shift perceptions of a change from "We don't have time to do this!" to "We don't have time to not do this". However, watch out also for any vested-interests, such as from vendors and others, not only in maintaining existing dysfunctionalities in current systems, but also in creating new ones within the intended transformation.

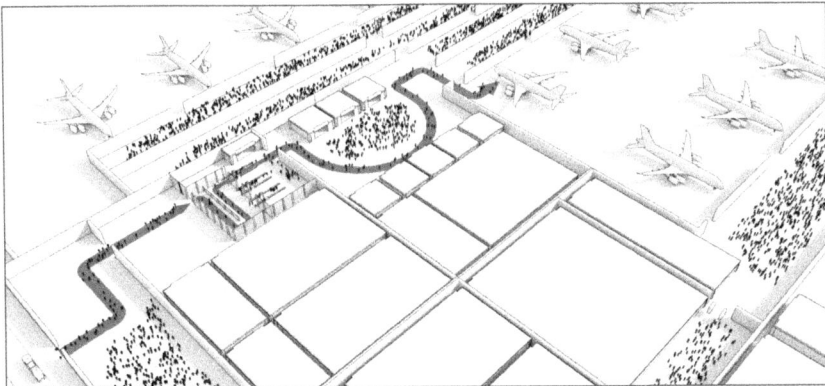

Limits and constraints. Although an airport wants to accept larger planes, it is limited by its current infrastructure.

9: Building-blocks for a viable business-architecture

What's the minimum that we need as a base for a viable business architecture?

This was part of a question sent to me by Chilean business-architect *Richard Moira Lupin*:

"What should a company have, what maturity, what capacity, what purposes, so that a business architect can, at least partially, exercise and execute business architecture projects?"

For various practical reasons, as you will see, it's probably most useful if I address each of those parts of that question in roughly the opposite order:

What is the purpose of business-architecture?

To me, the role of business-architecture is to build and maintain a clear picture of the structure and story that the organisation will need, in order to do its business. To maintain the architecture of *'the business of the business'*, in context of the organisation's market and the broader shared enterprise. And then help others use that picture to guide the implementation of that organisation's structures, services and operations, from a business perspective.

In functional terms, business-architecture sits as a bridge between strategy, product design, service-design, organisation-design, marketing and change-management. As well, some aspects of operations-design and knowledge-management.

The services that business-architecture would provide relate mainly to guidance for and arbitration between each of those organisational-functions above *(strategy, product-design etc)* for which it acts as a bridge, in relation to any questions about *'the business of the business'* as a unified whole.

The key effect of the absence of a distinct business-architecture is that business-analysts and others would be forced to make often random guesses about what *'the business of the business'* actually is. Such guesses are rarely consistent with each other, are often too easily influenced by vendors' *'solutioneering'*, and may well be incorrect.

What capacity for business-architecture will an organisation need?

It's probable that the only honest answer would be *'It depends...'*
The most common key factor here is organisational size and complexity.

For a small organisation addressing only a single market, the business-architecture is likely to be simple enough that it can be addressed as just one more minor task for the CEO or equivalent. By definition, all architectures are ultimately the responsibility of the CEO, though this responsibility is likely to be delegated to others in anything but the smallest of organisations.

As the business grows in scale and complexity, the need for a dedicated business-architecture role, and, later, a dedicated team, will increase. Probably the closest parallel would be the organisation's business-strategy function. A business-architecture team is likely to need to be roughly the same size as the strategy-team, though unlike strategists, business-architects are more likely to be a distributed-team working more directly with and between other business-functions.

What maturity will an organisation need before it can gain real value from business-architecture?

I would suggest that the correct answer is *'any maturity at all'.* For example, one of the times we most need a business-architecture is right at the start, when we have no organisational maturity at all. What differs at different levels of maturity is the emphases and priorities for the types of activities we need to undertake. We can use an *maturity-model* to guide us in this.

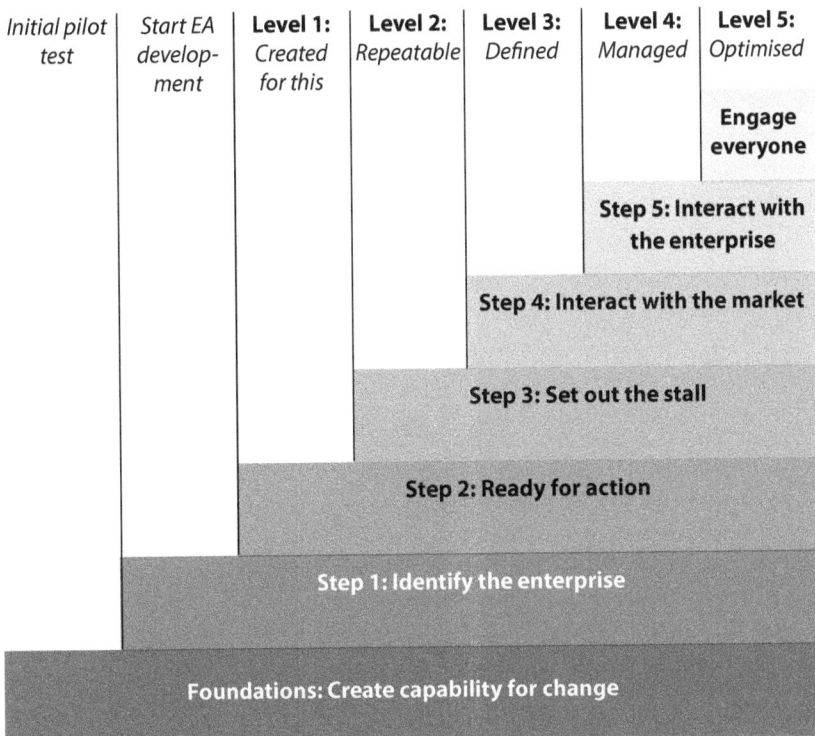

Initial pilot test	*Start EA development*	**Level 1:** *Created for this*	**Level 2:** *Repeatable*	**Level 3:** *Defined*	**Level 4:** *Managed*	**Level 5:** *Optimised*
						Engage everyone
					Step 5: Interact with the enterprise	
				Step 4: Interact with the market		
			Step 3: Set out the stall			
		Step 2: Ready for action				
	Step 1: Identify the enterprise					
Foundations: Create capability for change						

The **Maturity Model** can be used for Business Architecture.

Initial pilot test	Start EA develop-ment	**Level 1:** Created for this	**Level 2:** Repeatable	**Level 3:** Defined	**Level 4:** Managed	**Level 5:** Optimised

Engage everyone

Step 5: Pull together
Assessing across the whole airport

Step 4: Work with the real world
Staff say if all is working in airport.

Step 3: Set out the stall
Management and above make decisions, which affect the whole airport.

Step 2: Ready for action
Each department in airport assesses how they are functioning.

Step 1: Identify the enterprise
"We get people from outside the airport, through security to the correct plane, on time."

Foundations: Create capability for change
"We see areas where we can improve, such as in better signage".

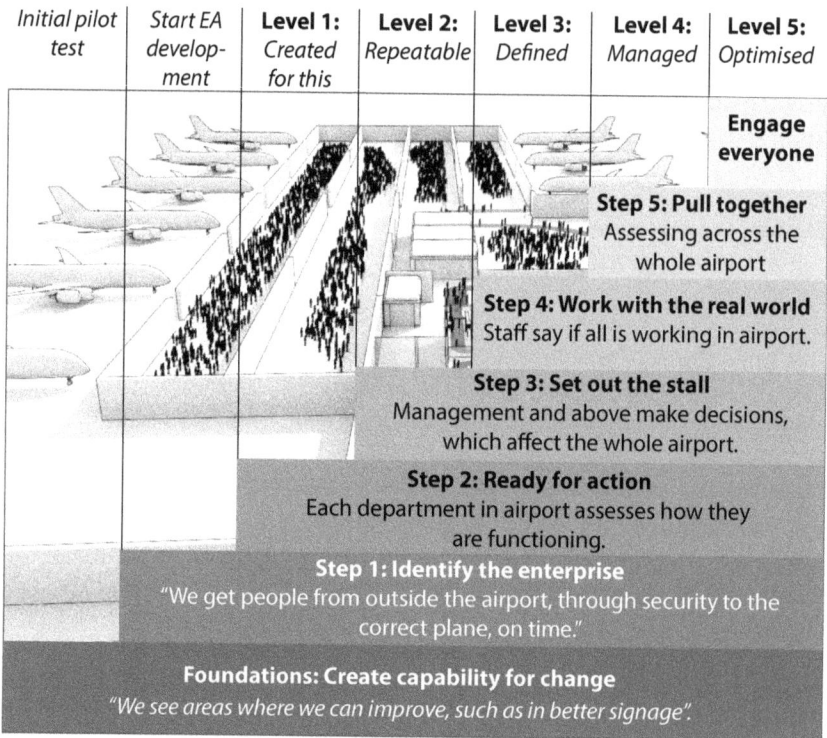

The **Maturity Model** used for the Business Architecture of an airport.

This *'maturity-map'* is not just a linear step-by-step sequence: we can do things *'out-of-sequence'* if we need to do so. Although it becomes harder to do, and almost certainly harder to maintain, if the maturity-level is not already well-established throughout the organisation.

What must a company have in place to support a successful and useful business-architecture?

I will presume that what is meant by *'have'* here is the set of artefacts, documents, diagrams, models and so on. These will be used to guide conversations on business-architecture and its use, dependent on the architecture purpose, capacity and maturity as above.

The single most important part of this top-level is the **'enterprise vision'**, a very brief summary, often no more than half a dozen words, about the *'what', 'how'* and *'why'* that holds the entire enterprise together. For this context, the term *'the enterprise'* is not the same as *'the organisation'*: it relates to the shared-enterprise that the organisation serves, and within which the organisation does its business. This is much broader in scope, not just broader than the organisation or even its market, but a scope bounded by a shared-story that would always continue to exist even if the organisation and market did not.

Values, success-criteria, standards, laws and regulations all devolve from that enterprise-vision, it is that important. The organisation then positions itself in relation to that enterprise, via its own mission and vision, which are necessarily lower than the enterprise vision itself, and not the other way round…

The enterprise-vision provides the anchor for looking *'outward'* from the organisation, towards its customers, suppliers, investors and other partners. We then need to link to that outward enterprise by looking *'inward'* into the organisation itself.

Therefore the other essential business-architecture tool, to aid with this, is the **capability-model** (*sometimes known by other terms such as 'Functional Business Model'*). This describes what the organisation does, in a deliberately abstract way. The capabilities or functions that are needed for the organisation to do its business, as distinct how those capabilities or functions are implemented at the present time. At its simplest possible level (*'Tier 1'*), almost every business-organisation would have a capability-model, describing that, looking something like below.

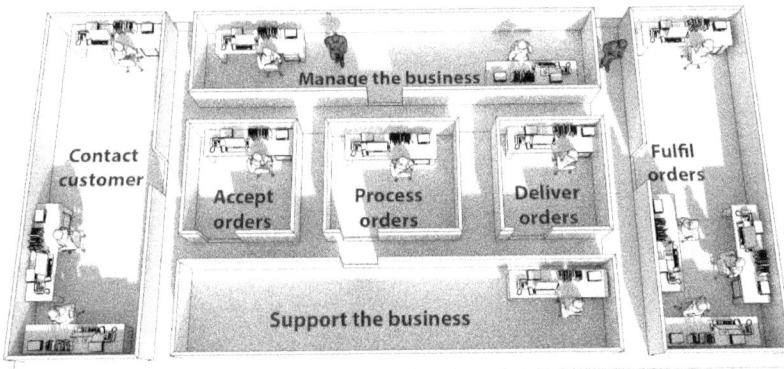

A Tier 1 capability model, describing in basic terms what an organisation does.

At the next level of detail (*'Tier 2'*), there's more differentiation, though organisations in the same industry would share a similar capability-map, to which industry-wide standards are often associated.

In business-architecture, we would typically develop our capability model to at least *'Tier-3'*, a more organisation-specific level, at which point it becomes of great use to the organisation.

Another useful business-architecture tactic is to use abstract context-neutral templates that can be adapted to context-specific needs.

For example, the service-based *Enterprise Canvas*[1] frame can be used as a simple and useful capability-model in its own right, that also helps to map out how a given service would link to the broader shared-enterprise.

1. See *Tools for Change-mapping, page 18*, for more details.

With the items mentioned, you should have the minimum you would need, to start developing a useful business-architecture.

There's one important condition related to all of the above. The concept of *'business-architecture'* described above is not the same as *'business-architecture'* in some *'enterprise'*-architecture frameworks.

In both approaches, *'business-architecture'* is regarded as a somewhat specialist sub-domain of a broader *'enterprise-architecture'*.
But that is almost the only similarity between the two approaches.

In the approach described here, *'business-architecture'* is a literal *'the architecture of the organisation's business',* in context of *'enterprise-architecture'* as a literal *'the architecture of the enterprise'*.
The focus of attention in each architecture is always *'people-first',* not *'technology-first'*: technologies may be important, but only ever as an enabler in context of the business and the enterprise itself.

However, in other IT-focused *'enterprise'*-architecture frameworks, the emphasis is typically the other way round: *'technology-first',* rather than *'people-first'*. Any people-concerns are below those of the technology.

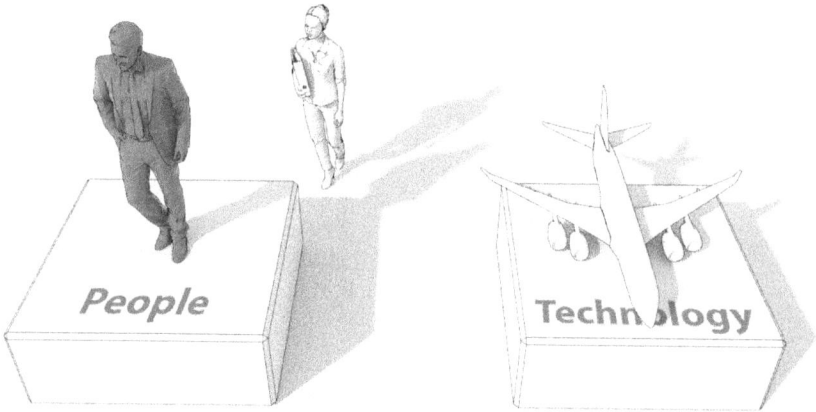

The focus of attention in each architecture should be 'people-first',
not 'technology-first' in context of the business and the enterprise itself.

10: Marketing and the service-oriented enterprise

As the economy shifts from manufacturing toward services, how do marketing and market-relationships need to change with this shift? And what enterprise-architectures do we need to support this?

As *Dave Gray* indicated in his article *'Everything is a service',* many people in and around business are seeing a *'Great Reset',* a fundamental shift in the nature of the economy, and with it a fundamental shift in the nature of a viable business: a change in focus from products to services.

In a product-oriented economy, an organisation's market is built around transactions, exchanges of goods and services. Within this metaphor, services are *almost*-products, another type of *'thing'* to be *'consumed'* by a passive marketplace of *'consumers'.* Financial services, for example, are packaged as *'products'.* So-called service organisations sell *'solutions'* to often-unspecified 'problems' that a *'consumer'* is presumed to face.

Producers produce, consumers consume: the roles are explicit, and explicitly separate and distinct. The role of marketing there is to create a market *'want',* often entirely artificial, for whatever product the producers wish to sell. The role of enterprise-architecture and the like is to support creation of the maximum volume of product for the minimum necessary effort and cost.

The overall view, perhaps illustrated best by the *Business Model Canvas,* is a linear structure of processes. A supply-chain feeds into the business-processes of the organisation, the results of which are then sold on to *'consumers'.* The sequence ends at the *'consumer',* at the moment that the customer has paid for the *'product';* and everything is centred around the organisation, as *'the enterprise'.*

This view of the market is also often possession-based, with very unequal power-relationships assumed between the organisation and everyone else: we talk about *'capturing'* a market, *'owning'* market-share, and so on. This often leads in turn to a very combative relationship across the market, both between organisations competing for *'possession'* of market-share, and between an organisation and its customers, employees and broader communities. All of whom, unsurprisingly, may well object to being treated as possessed *'objects'* or *'subjects'* of the organisation.

In business terms, one of the key drivers behind the *'big reset'* or *'big shift'* that *Dave Gray* describes is that this model of the market is rapidly becoming less and less viable. Most markets are either at or approaching saturation-point; the hidden-costs are becoming more visible, and harder to externalise; and the supposed economies of scale of mass-production and mass-marketing deliver steadily lower returns, especially relative to smaller and more adaptable technologies and business-models. And in economic terms, there are practical limits as to how much *'stuff'* we can continue to make and sell on a finite planet. Some real problems there and yet they are a solid part of that model of the business-market.

A service-oriented economy is radically different, in that the market is built primarily around relationships.

Everyone in the market is both *'producer'* and *'consumer'*: the roles blur, and are much more equal or peer-based in nature than in the product-oriented economy.

This view of the market is also based much more on mutual responsibilities: we talk about co-creation, about partnering in a shared enterprise. The power-relationships are much more equal, and necessarily focussed on building and maintaining mutual trust, rather than the combative contracts of the possession-model, which mostly reflect an absence of trust.

The overall model still has transactions and processes and supply-chains, but the perspective is different. As *Verna Allee* describes it, that linear *'supply-chain'* is actually one view into a much more complex *'value-network'*. And a product-transaction or service-transaction is merely one phase within a much larger market-cycle:

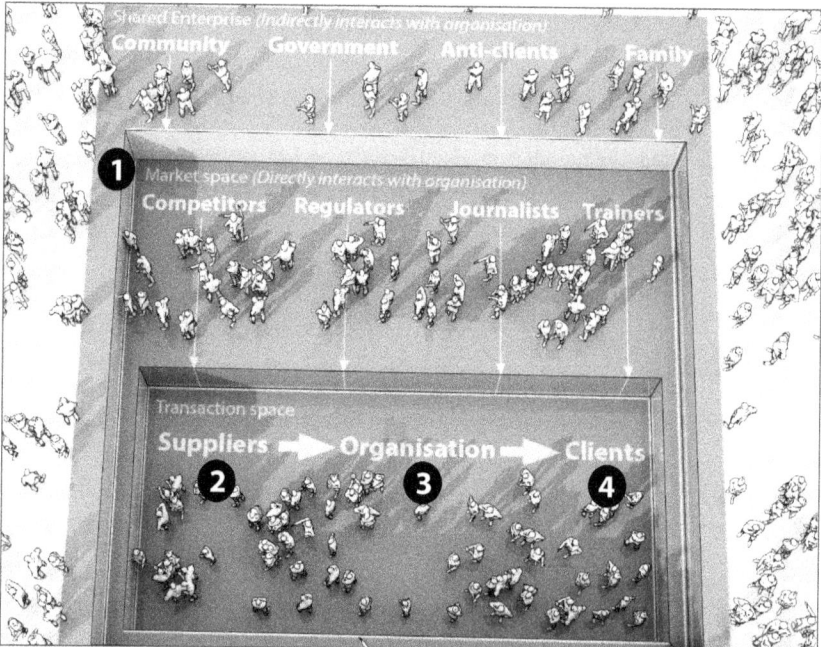

1 *A market space defines a set of roles in relation to a vision.* **2** *The Suppliers for the value-proposition.* **3** *An organisation offers a value-proposition, aligned to the vision in a market role, delivered via a mission, validated via goals.* **4** *Clients/Customers for the value-proposition.*

Importantly, the fundamental focus of relationships is inverted, from organisation-focused to customer-focused. The sales-focus also shifts from 'push' to 'pull', from manipulating or even forcing the 'consumer' into a single once-off 'the sale', to building a continuing long-term mutual relationship. All of this requires radically different approaches to sales and marketing, but it can be done, and increasingly, is much more profitable than the 'push' model.

For example, compare your experience of the typical time-driven 'customer-as-product' sales call-centre, to an intentionally relationship-oriented call-centre which focusses much more on respect and mutual trust. Which approach would you prefer to deal with in your business day? The answer's fairly obvious: which is why the conventional call-centre model is becoming less and less viable, no matter how much pressure is put upon the long-suffering staff.

Another first-hand example: a couple days ago I was looking at cameras in the local branch of a medium-sized national chain of camera-stores. The absence of pressure was really noticeable; and the saleswoman's quiet passion for photography shone through. The change in energy of the place was very noticeable, compared to the last time I had been there, a year or so ago.

Talking with her, it became clear that the company had made that crucial shift from **product-orientation** to **service-orientation**. The key was that they had come to understand they made most of their money not from selling cameras, but from the ongoing photo-print service. Camera-sales became viewed as a means to support that service: it needed to be profitable in its own right, but it wasn't the primary focus for profit. It had became much more important to match the camera to the client's actual needs. And that emphasis on matching real needs itself became a key foundation for mutual trust, and therefore the long-term relationships that would be profitable to all parties.

Contrast that with the usual high-street high-pressure retailer, where the emphasis is more likely to be about off-loading the highest-margin object that the 'consumer' could afford, then dropping the attention instantly so as to move on to the next 'customer' as quickly as possible. "I worked in a place like that for three months", she said, "and I felt like I aged ten years while I was there. Soul-destroying, for everyone."

So what kind of enterprise-architecture do we need for a service-oriented enterprise? How does it differ from the conventional product-oriented architectures, particularly in its business-architecture and process-architecture? Probably the key requirement is an awareness of the implications of one simple statement:

A service exists to serve.

But what does it serve? And whom does it serve? Architecturally, those are not trivial questions…

In the highly unequal power-relationships in the conventional product-oriented model, the answers are very clear indeed: there is often a thin pretence of *'customer-service',* but in reality the *'consumer'* is seen to exist only to serve the organisation and its perceived *'need'* to sell.

And the organisation in turn is deemed to exist only to serve the *'needs'* of the stockholders, but that is another story…

But in a service-oriented enterprise, there are two fundamentally different types of service going on: and the architecture needs to support both of these.

One type, which we might describe as *'horizontal',* is the conventional *'supply-chain'* structure: the service-producer serves the needs of the service-consumer. The issues here that the architecture needs to support are that:
- *the relationships between producer and consumer are essentially peer-to-peer*
- *the roles of 'producer' and 'consumer' will often blur or even swap over, especially in the 'co-creation' relationships that are common in a service-oriented model*
- *the overall relationships are built via the self-reinforcing loop of the full 'market-cycle', as above*

The other type of service is more *'vertical'*: within the context of those *'horizontal'* supply-chain service-relationships, every player in the shared-enterprise serves the same overall vision and values.
The market exists within the context of a broader shared-enterprise, defined by a distinct purpose or *'vision'* and its associated values.

There is a crucial difference here between the organisation and those with whom it interacts. Architecturally speaking, the organisation chooses the vision and values to which it will align.
When customers' experiences, and suppliers' experiences, happen also to align with that same vision and values, there is then a basis for a shared connection. Serving the same ends, the same vision and values, creates the basis for mutual trust, which then starts the market-cycle rolling.

So the service is delivered through the *'horizontal'* connection; but the connection only exists because both parties share *'vertical'* alignment to the same vision and values.

Note that the customers' experiences, or even supplier's experiences, may only align with the organisation's chosen vision for a brief period.

But while that alignment exists, there is the basis for conversation and connection, and so the first stage of the market-cycle already in progress.

Back to the camera-shop. First, there was a conversation, which in some stores doesn't even happen at all. And the conversation didn't have an all-too-obvious undercurrent of: *'How can we sell you a high-priced camera that you don't need?'* Instead, I felt listened-to, respected, safe, served, all of which increases the likelihood that I would go back there when I am ready to buy another camera. In other words, that first part of the market-cycle is already in progress; and I feel safe in the belief that the closing *'post-sale'* part of the market-cycle would be there, too.

Yet note that I wouldn't go there to buy anything that wasn't about cameras, because that isn't part of their vision or purpose that they present. They are clear about what they do and what they don't do, and demonstrate their vision and values in practice. So I know when to go there, and when not to go there. Sounds obvious, perhaps: but some organisations are so sales obsessed that they give the impression that they will sell us anything, whether they have it or not, just to make up their sales-quota.

Architecturally, the vision and values are the core of a service-oriented architecture: everything in the organisation needs to be understood as serving that vision.

For this reason, for example, the value of a service-viability checklist that explicitly includes tracing of support for each of the values as they touch on every aspect of the enterprise.

Also the importance of ensuring that that same vision is carried across any partner or outsourcing-relationships, especially where key customer-facing connections are handled by outsourced others such as an external customer-service centre.

Note that the customers' experiences, or even supplier's experiences, may only align with the organisation's chosen vision for a brief period.

○○○○○ *Taken from the chapter: **Marketing and the service-oriented enterprise***

11: The balance between usefulness and profit

One of the constant challenges for enterprise-architecture, probably all forms of architecture, in fact, is explaining the value of what we do. For example, like a good conference-organiser or event-host, often the better we do our work, the less visible it becomes. Often the only way we can see this invisible work in an enterprise is when two or more business-teams are claiming credit for the same thing: for that to happen, it means that there's a good architecture there that created the otherwise-invisible bridge between them.

Yet how do we make the invisible more visible, without doing so by showing up only its failings? One option might be to go back to a very old description of much the same kind of theme, *Lao Tse's Tao Te Ching*[1]:

"Thirty spokes share the wheel's hub;
It is the centre hole that makes it useful.
Shape clay into a vessel;
It is the space within it that makes it useful.
Cut doors and windows for a room;
It is the holes which make it useful.
Therefore profit comes from what is there;
Usefulness from what is not there."

Both *'profit'* and *'usefulness'* twist and turn continually around each other. The two need to balance each other, support each other; and each also contains elements of the other, a point that we could illustrate with yet another ancient image: the *yin* and *yang* symbol.

The Yin and Yang symbol.

1. *Lao Tse's Tao Te Ching, Chapter 11,* translation by Gia Fu Feng and Jane English

The danger is that many people in business will focus only on the *'profit'* part, and ignore the rest. And even if they don't fall for that mistake, there is still a tendency for *'usefulness'* to become lost in the shadows. If we over-focus on the *'profit'* side of the balance, the *'usefulness'* quietly fades away into nothingness, and with it, over time, the profit too.

Which is where the need for architecture comes into the picture, to create a better balance between *'what is there'* and *'what is not there'.* The balance between *'profit-centres'* and *'cost-centres'*, for example, and to make the hidden visible again. The catch, of course, is that architecture itself is a function that focusses mostly on *'usefulness'*, on overall effectiveness, which is perhaps why some at first fail to see much profit in it.

One way to resolve that would be to note that while most of the business tends to focus on profit, architecture tends to counter that over-focus by placing its focus on usefulness, because without usefulness, there is no profit.

It is also true that without profit there would probably be no usefulness, although we should note also that *'profit'* may take many different forms.

In that sense, it's very much in business' interest to make the invisible become visible, otherwise they can't tell where their profit comes from, and therefore where it may go again, without warning.

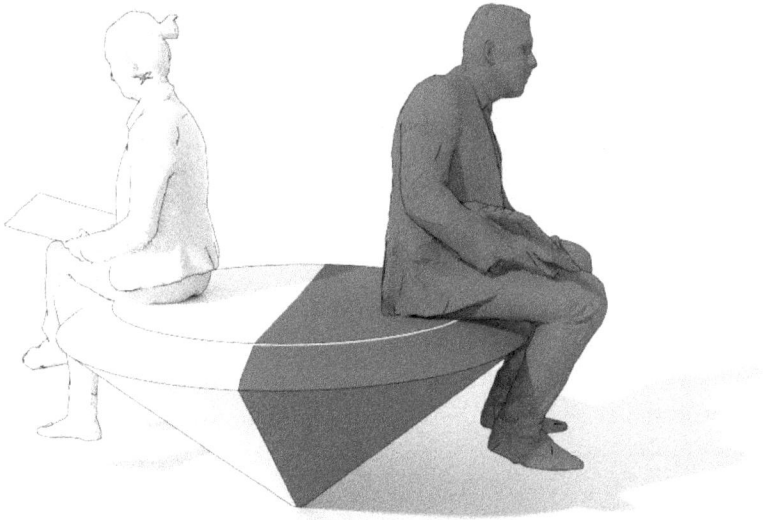

The balance between profit and usefulness.

⬠⬠⬠⬠⬠ *Taken from the chapter:* **Architecting the balance between usefulness and profit**

12: Working with the shadows

In enterprise-architecture, we have long known about the importance of shadow-IT, the place where much of business IT-innovation comes from, yet also presents organisational risks if not managed appropriately.

At my workshop at the Irish Computer Society, the conversation shifted to the relationship between *'fintech' (financial-technology)* start-ups and the insurance companies that acquire them. And from somewhere between us, up came the idea of shadow-business-model. It is much the same as shadow-IT, but in this case the *'hands-off'* relationship allows the receiver to experiment with business-models, separate from many of the reputational, regulatory and other constraints that would and should apply to the organisation's main business-model.

Another example was a large online retailer's acquisition of a product manufacturer, companies with very different cultures. Yet very different business-models and operating-models, but where a careful *'hands-off'* relationship allowed each to learn from the other.

In SCAN terms, we could summarise the generic positioning of all *'shadow'* functions, shadow-IT, shadow-business-models, shadow-management and more as follows:

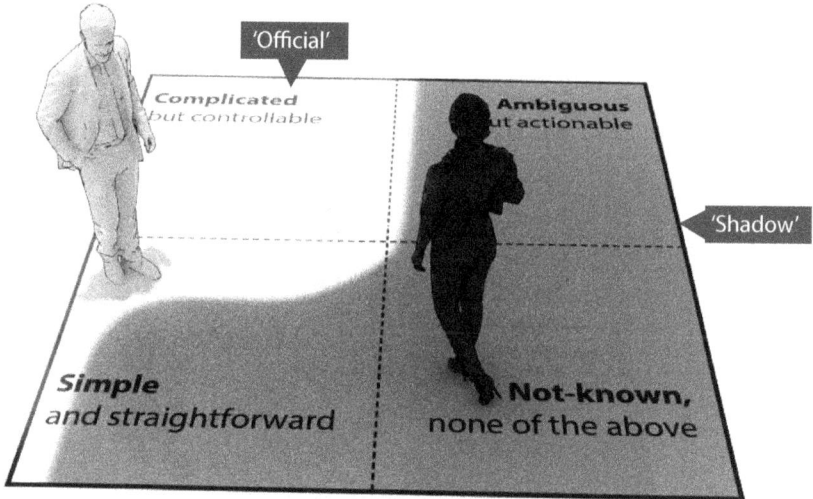

A simplified version of the SCAN tool showing the positioning of all 'shadow functions'.

In other words, the *'shadow'*-world exists to deal with and resolve all the uncertainties and over-simplifications that overly-mechanistic management models tend to overlook.

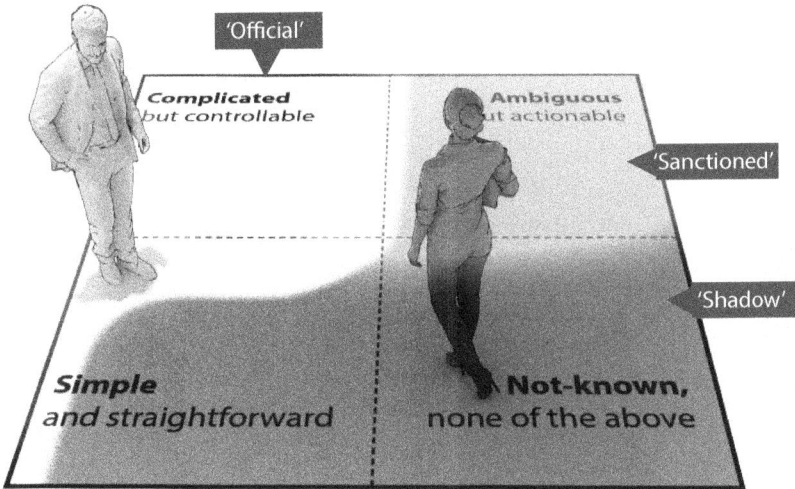

When some exploration of the uncertain is officially sanctioned, the shadow-world still needs to exist.

Even in more aware management-models, in which some exploration of the uncertain is officially sanctioned and allowed, the shadow-world will still always need to exist, particularly whenever the work gets closer towards real-time action, as shown above.

From an enterprise-architecture viewpoint, the *'shadow'*-world needs that separation from the *'official channels'* in order to do its job properly. That is the point that's easy to miss. The shadow elements deal with the parts of the context *(and its architecture)* that the *'official channels'* can not address, because they, by definition, only deal with a world of certainty. For example, by definition, innovation can only occur with something that's not-known, beyond the rules, literally anarchic. If we try to force the *'shadow'* elements to be *'under control',* or bring them all *'out into the light',* we defeat the whole object of the exercise.

Instead, it's best to think more in terms of a spectrum of *'governance-of-governance',* and the *'shadow'*-elements need to be right out at the far end of that spectrum, under a much looser form of governance.

The danger or risk, of course, as can be seen so easily with misuse of shadow-IT, is if there can too easily be a disconnect from or to the big-picture strategy. Therefore the importance of commanders'-intent to provide the core guidance within that looser form of governance . Also the *auftragstaktik*[1]*/fingerspitzengefühl*[2] feedback-loop that helps maintain situational awareness under turbulent change *(see overleaf).*

1.Auftragstaktik
A set of military tactics focusing on initiative and flexibility.
2. Fingerspitzengefühl
In brief, describing good situational awareness.

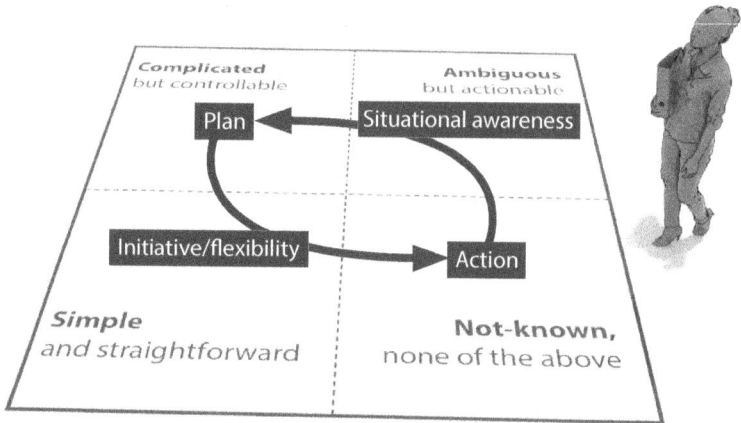

Maintaining situational awareness under turbulent change.

For architects, the catch is that that loop is crucially dependent on many themes and factors that would be completely invisible to a mainstream IT-focussed *'enterprise'*-architecture. Themes such as person-to-person connection, sensing, *'feel'* and, above all, trust.

To ensure that the *'shadow'*-elements work well for the enterprise, and are appropriately covered in the organisation's structured *'governance of governance',* enterprise-architects must explicitly include and incorporate those *'hidden'* themes into the architecture.

As the literal *'the architecture of the enterprise',* a real enterprise-architecture must cover every aspect of the enterprise, including all of the *'shadow'*-elements. And yet, those *'shadow'*-elements cannot be brought *'under control',* not least because they deal with the themes and factors that are beyond the reach of conventional concepts of *'control'.* We need to acknowledge their existence, learn to work with them, and yet also allow them to remain somewhat *'in the shadows'.*

13: Business is social

Business is a social enterprise, to quote the FEAF / IEEE-1471 definition:

"An enterprise is an organisation or cross-functional entity supporting a defined business scope or mission… It includes interdependent resources, people, organisations, technology, who must coordinate their functions and share information in support of a common mission or set of related missions".

The *"common mission or set of related missions"* provide the purpose for the transformations, transactions, relations and conversations: without that, the business literally has no purpose. And that shared-purpose in turn defines value, what is valued *(and, for that matter, what is not valued)* in each of those transactions and conversations and suchlike. Each enterprise is different, and is anchored in different values: so concepts such as *'competitive advantage'* are relevant only for enterprises that compete with each other, and may make no sense at all in others *(such as government)* that usually don't.

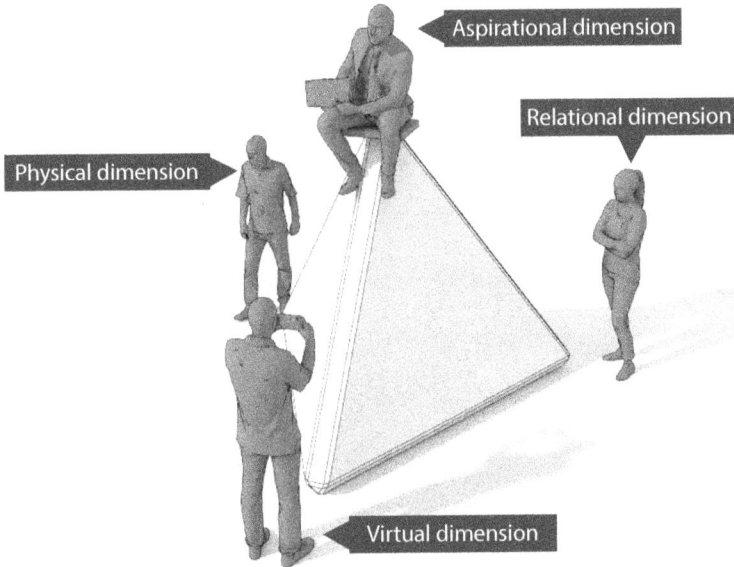

The Tetradian, with four distinct dimensions.

As I have explored before, what we are actually dealing with here is a *'tetradian',* a set of four distinct dimensions that, together, encompass the architecture of the enterprise:
- *physical 'things'*
- *virtual information and imagined space*
- *relations between people*
- *aspirations for individual and shared purpose, the definition of the enterprise itself*

 Taken from the chapter: **Business is social, business as purpose**

14: What is a shared enterprise?

What exactly is *'the enterprise'* in enterprise-architecture? To what extent is that enterprise a shared-enterprise? And how does this affect enterprise-architecture itself?

In reality each of those questions is fundamental to enterprise-architecture, and the way we choose to answer them will in turn affect both how we view the role of EA in business and elsewhere, and how we address it as a practice.

First, the term **enterprise**. Its literal root, from French, is *'between take'* (French: *'entre'*, between; *'prendre'*, take), hence entrepreneur as a literal *'between-taker'* who takes on a role as active intermediary placing itself between needs.

Enterprise describing both aim or intent, often indicated via a story, and also of the energy or drive to reach towards that aim, to engage in that story.

To reach towards that aim, we are likely to need to organise and provide some kind of structure around which to gather resources and coordinate actions towards that aim. *'Organisation is the verb, the activity, which in turn leads to 'the organisation'* as noun, the structures arising from that activity; all of which arise in context of and because of *the-enterprise-as-aim*. Note again that although *'organisation'* and *'enterprise'* are closely intertwined here, they are not the same. The simplest summary would be that organisation is *'how'*, enterprise is *'why'*.

As the ambitions of enterprise grow in scope and scale, so too must the organisation. Which, if we've already made the common mistake of blurring together *'organisation'* and *'enterprise'*, in turn leads to the common idea that *'enterprise'* means *'a large commercial organisation'*. An enterprise as a descriptor of scale, rather than of aim or intent. Leading to the all too common view that enterprise-architecture is relevant only to large commercial organisations. Yet by definition, *enterprise-as-intent* can and does apply at any scope or scale, so the same must apply to any architecture of that enterprise. It is best to not use the *enterprise-as-scale* concept as the basis for *'enterprise'* in enterprise-architecture: it is guaranteed to mislead.

What about the term *architecture*? Again, many different interpretations, typically more dependent on content, such as data-architecture, naval-architecture, and so on.

Enterprise-architecture is a bit different, in that its content is *other* architectures: it's more of a *meta-architecture*[1], less focussed on content,

---

1. *An architecture for making architecture. A template you will adapt when context is added. You can compare parts from different architectures*

more on how to link other architectures together, within the overall context of the organisation and enterprise. One way to put it is that we build an *'enterprise-architecture'* of and for an organisation, in context of and about the enterprise that drives the actions for that organisation.

Which in turn is where *'shared-enterprise'* comes into the picture.

'Shared-enterprise' means is that there is some aspect of enterprise, that is held not just by us, but by others too. Which always occurs, because there are always interactions with others about the matter of the enterprise. Which means that to understand and model the interactions of our organisation with that enterprise, our enterprise-architecture will need to understand and model the shared aspects of each of those interactions with others in the shared-enterprise.
Amongst other things, that tells us the drivers, the *'why'*, for each of the interactions. Without that, it would be all but impossible to make sense of those interactions, or even what some of those interactions are doing, such as placing our organisation at risk.
Which is why this matters to enterprise-architecture.

Also what is shared are the elements that indicate an enterprise, namely vision, values and commitments. Typically expressed as aims, drivers, story, definitions of success or not-success, definitions of *'right'* and *'wrong'*, and more. Note that this is significantly different from an organisation, which is bounded by rules, roles and responsibilities, another reason why blurring *'organisation'* and *'enterprise'* will lead to problems.

If we don't explore the shared-enterprise, we would be basing all of our designs and processes for interactions with others upon random, untested assumptions. Note too the crucial difference between interactions within the organisation[1] versus interactions with others beyond the organisation[2]. Being clear about those differences is crucial for validity and viability of any enterprise-architecture, and for all other domain-architectures too

When attempting to model a shared enterprise there is an important catch. If we have placed the organisation as the apparent centre of the shared-enterprise, that is the correct thing to do when we are modelling those interactions from the organisation's perspective. But when we need to position the organisation in context of its competitors or collaborators in a more complex market-relationship, we will need a different view of that same pattern, one that is not centred *only* on our organisation.

---

1. *Which we can attempt to control with rules and so on, but for which we would be wise to base much on enterprise-drivers too.*
2. *Which we cannot 'control', but only influence, via our understanding of the shared aspects of the enterprise.*

As soon as we place ourselves in a shared-enterprise, the enterprise of *'business-travel'*. in this example below, we automatically place ourselves in relation to and with every other player in that shared-enterprise. Each of those players would no doubt see themselves as the centre of their own relationships and interactions with others in that market and the broader shared-enterprise. And correctly so, if only in the sense that each organisation has its own responsibilities in how it interacts with others in that shared-enterprise. Every player affects and is affected by every other player, sometimes with potentially-huge impacts on business and more. This includes risks, and opportunities, that would be utterly invisible unless we take the deliberate care to bring them to the surface. It is only if we do have a solid grasp of what the shared-enterprise is, and how expectations and interactions flow around within it, that we and our organisation can start to have some real choices about those impacts.

Without a solid understanding of shared-enterprise, an *'enterprise'*-architecture cannot be either valid or viable as *'the architecture of the enterprise'*, and so itself also places the viability of the organisation at risk.

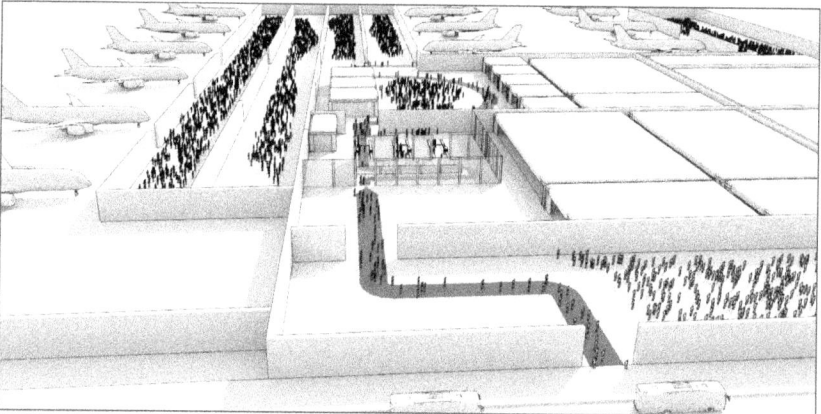

A shared enterprise of 'business-travel, made up of players, each placing themselves at the centre of the shared-enterprise. Including airlines, passengers and the airport itself.

15: The enterprise of travel

If the key role of enterprise-architecture is that things work better when they work together, on purpose, how do we make that happen? And what happens when they don't?

In our example a disgruntled passenger is struggling with an international airline's response to their complaint, via social media, *(The specific details have been altered, but it is based on a real event).*
Bert was stuck at the wrong airport, trying to contact the customer helpline for more than an hour, leading to understandable dissatisfaction with the airline and their customer support.
Later the customer empathised with the airline's employees, who were stuck using IT systems which didn't allow them to do anything.
I commented about this online and was unimpressed to receive this response from the airline:

Airline: @tetradian Sorry for the long wait Tom, our team are experiencing high call volumes. Let us know if we can help via this channel. Betty.

In principle, yes, it was nice, respectful, it showed that they were listening out on social-media, and providing information, or at least an excuse, of sorts, from a real person rather than a robot. All of which would have been great if it had been me, rather than Bert, that was stuck on the customer-*'service'* call-queue. Since I wasn't, it was sort-of *"Right idea, wrong person"*, which, if anything, compounded the offence.

And it still doesn't resolve the deeper problem that is the real point here.

So let's look at that real problem.

To make sense of what went wrong, and what we need to do about it, there appear to be four main themes:
• *failure to understand the customer-needs and customer-journey*
• *failure to counteract against organisation-centric system design*
  Conway's Law[1]
• *failure to design for uncertainty and complexity in the context*
• *failure to fully connect across outsource-boundaries (although this theme might not apply in this specific case)*

All of these themes interweave with each other in ways that are often completely invisible in an organisation-centric view, but can be all too painfully evident in the customer-experience.

---

1. Conway's Law
"Organisations which design systems are constrained to produce designs which are copies of the communication structures of these organisations."
Melvin E. Conway (Wikipedia)

And those painful experiences can create *anticlient*[1]-type relationships, which are not good for the organisation…

So let's briefly explore each of these in turn, and then link them all together.

Customer-needs and customer-journey

For this one, we need to understand the different perspectives on the organisation and the broader enterprise, and, in particular, the interactions as seen *'inside-out'* versus *'outside-in'*:

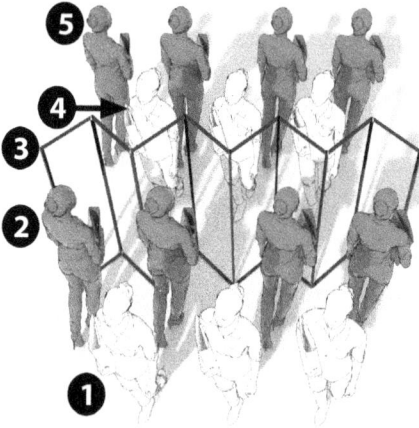

A 3D view of the Inside-out/inside in model.

As a quick summary:

1 Inside-in

The world is viewed as if the organisation is the only thing that exists.
We need this view in order to focus on internal efficiency and suchlike.

2 Inside-out

The world is viewed as though it exists to serve the needs of the organisation.
We need this view in order to determine how to present and execute an offer of a product or service to other players in the shared-enterprise.

3 Interaction journey

The interaction between the organisation and the client/customer.

4 Outside-in

The organisation is viewed as if it may be something that the world needs.
We need this view in order to identify what other players within the enterprise actually want, and how to interact with them.

5 Outside-out

Is the 'world' in its own terms, whether or not the organisation exists.
We need this view in order to identify the values within the enterprise.

1.Anti-client

A client/customer who is dissatisfied with an organisations service/product.
Sometimes so much so that they can become quite vocal to others about their dissatisfaction.

What is often known as the *customer-journey* takes place between *'outside-in' (what the customer needs and expects from the organisation)* and *'inside-out' (what the organisation needs and expects from the customer).*

To understand what actually happens in those interactions, and so design for an optimum balance between the players, we need to use techniques such as *customer-journey mapping.*

If we don't do this, we end up with random guesses about what others want from us, how they feel, and more.

For example, it's very easy to forget that, in these contexts, *feelings* are often the key facts that we need to work with. There's also a very common tendency to assume that others *'should'* do what we expect. Should always interact with us in the ways that are easiest for us rather than for them. But reality is that they don't, and we need to design for those facts, rather than pretend that they don't exist.

Organisation-centric system-design

If we don't pay attention to that balance between *inside-out* and *outside-in*, and to the very different emphases that we would need so as to support a customer-journey well, what we are likely to end up with is a system that is almost entirely built around *inside-out* and *inside-in*. In other words, with all interactions built around the ways that the organisation views the world, and views itself. And which, in turn, will almost certainly align with *Conway's Law.* Meaning that:

- *if the organisation is based around silos, the structures of its systems will reflect those silos*
- *if the organisation does not communicate well across its silos, then neither will the resulting systems or processes*
- *anyone who uses the systems must learn to think about the context in the same way that the organisation thinks about the context and about itself*
- *anyone who uses the systems must themselves compensate and adapt for any communication-gaps within the organisation's systems*

Silo-based information-structures and processes can create terrible problems, through all manner of missed-connections. We also get spiralling fragmentation of continuity from splitting up a domain into ever-smaller specialisms. Unless we take deliberate action to reduce these *'natural'* tendencies in system-design, we will end up with systems that are all but unusable, especially when we try to offload much of the integration-work onto our customers, as we would typically expect to do in any so-called *'digital'* business-model.

In many organisations, the situation is so bad that, in effect, customers need to know more about the organisation's structures, information-systems and processes than the organisation knows about itself, just in order to get their needs met at all. And it's not just customers who are affected: the same all too often applies to employees trying to make sense of and with their own organisation's systems on behalf of customers, or to do any cross-silo connections, such as the in-person customer-service officer trying to disentangle an accounts-problem for me at her bank.

Complexity and uncertainty

Most IT-systems are transactional: they deal with the same kind of thing in the same predictable way, over and over, and, if well-designed, they may be very good at it. Which is all well and good, for those parts of the context that are predictable, and do always remain the same. For those that aren't or don't, not so good. And there lies a rather serious problem that many people often don't seem able even to see…

IT-systems work well with order, predictability, certainty. In most cases, they don't work well, if at all, with disorder, unpredictability, uncertainty, and the *out of the ordinary*. The catch is that any real-world context will always contain a mix of all of those elements, order and disorder, predictable and unpredictable, certain and uncertain. Which means that if we want a real-world system to work well, it needs to able to cope with pretty much anything that the real-world cares to throw at it, and not just *'the easy bits'*, repeatable, predictable, certain.

At this point we also need to note the distinctions between tame-problems and wild-problems *(or wicked problems)*. Tame-problems are ones that have a definite solution, that generally remain the same every time we encounter them. IT-systems work really well with tame-problems.
What IT-systems don't work well with are wild-problems, ones that don't stay the same, that typically need unique solutions, and that are always a bit uncertain, unpredictable, *'new'.* And the real-world always contains a mix of tame-problems and wild-problems, with the latter much more common in real-world action than many managers would like to admit.

The key point here is that most of the questions that arrive at customer service are likely to be wild-problems. That is because, these days, most customers, will have already resolved any tame-problems themselves, via all of any good airline's standard IT-based services, such as FAQs.

So if they call customer-service, it's because they have already exhausted all the tame-problem options.

At that point, they need a real person to help them sort out a real wild-problem, one that can't be resolved by tame-problem means.

Which means that they are likely already feeling frustrated before they even call the service-line.

So one thing not to do at this point is to dump the customer into a lengthy, costly call-queue with no indication of what is going on.

A queue that arises, we note, only because the company concerned hasn't understood the need for *necessary-fuzziness[1]* in customer-service system-designs. Or, worse, expects their customers to navigate the company's *'efficient'*, but-ineffective so-called *'support'*.

Pretending that everything in customer-service *'should'* be a tame-problem, simply because it seems simpler for us to deal with that way, will lead to problems

Connect across outsource boundaries

This one didn't apply in the airline's case, but it is all too common elsewhere. The wide range of disservice-risks that arise whenever we set out to outsource customer-service.

The problem here revolves around a crucial distinction that I usually describe as *'boundary of identity versus boundary of control'.*
In particular, the key concern here is that from a customer's perspective, an outsourced service is inside the organisation's boundary of identity but outside of its boundary of control. What this means in practice is that if the outsourced-service screws up, it's the organisation that takes the blame, not the outsourced-service.

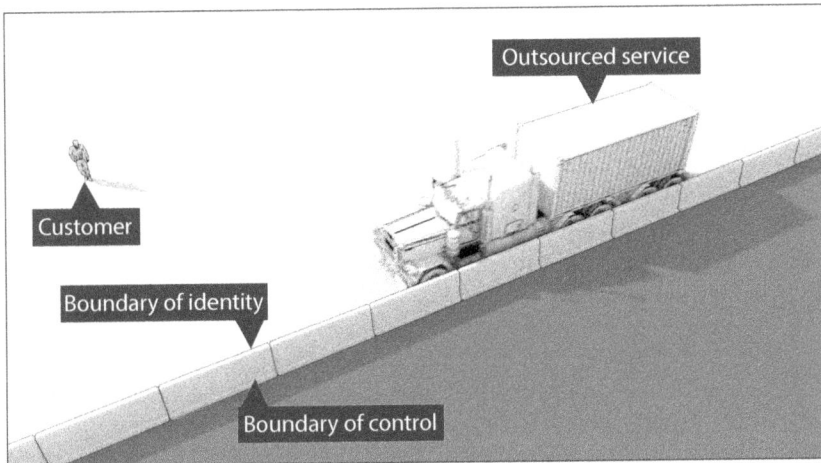

From a customer's perspective, an outsourced service is inside the organisation's boundary of identity but outside of its boundary of control.

Because the whole point is that, in terms of the customer's experience, the outsourcer *'is'* the organisation.
For most organisations, they seem to assume that outsourcing is merely about predictable transactions under predictable rules.
But in reality it's about a lot more than just that.

---

1. Necessary-fuzziness
Describes and determines the amount of leeway and allowance for uncertainty that must be built into a system.

In outsourcing, the outsourcer represents the organisation, every aspect of the organisation. Including relationships, reputation, brand, trust and more. If the outsourcer screws up, it is the organisation's relationship, reputation, brand, trust and more that are on the line. And the outsourcer not **may**, but **will** screw up if they don't know *(or care about)* the values and so on that underpin the enterprise-story within which the organisation operates.

So if the organisation doesn't provide that information about brands and values and so on, and the training to support that information and why it is important to the organisation, the outsourcer **will** screw up at some point, with a high probability of damage to the organisation. But such things are rarely included in an outsourcing contract. Even for contexts such as customer-service, where high-uncertainty wild-problems are likely.

The wiser guideline here is this: do not outsource anything that has a high probability of wild-problems. A standardised back-office process that never touches any real customer, supplier or everyday employees, for that matter? *Yes, sure, do it.*
An outbound call-centre that follows a standard script via a single standard system? *Yes, okay, if you must, though it's a really good way of creating a lot of anti-clients if you're not careful about it.*
But an inbound customer-service call-centre that has to deal with a lot complex wild-problems that can cross any organisational boundaries or silos? *Do **not** outsource it.*

Implications for enterprise-architecture
Providing proper support for customer-service and suchlike creates some significant challenges for enterprise-architecture.
The key concerns can be summarised as follows:
• *Always start from a customer-oriented view, using concepts and tools such customer-journey mapping.*
• *Accept that changing the organisation's systems to better support a customer-oriented view will almost certainly mandate challenges to existing organisational culture and structure, and that addressing such concerns is a necessary part of the architecture-work.*
• *Accept and acknowledge that customer-service is likely to involve higher levels of uncertainty, unpredictability, complexity and wild-problem contexts than elsewhere in the more transactional parts of the organisation's processes. And so are likely to need significantly different designs, processes and governance to support them.*
• *Accept and acknowledge that the necessary-fuzziness in the context will also likely require quite high levels of necessary-inefficiency in the support-systems, and that any attempts to trim below that level of necessary-inefficiency will risk damaging overall effectiveness.*
• *Wherever practicable, actively resist any pressures to outsource customer-service capabilities, using the architectural reasons above to explain why any apparent financial-benefits from such outsourcing would be greatly outweighed by the hidden risks from doing so.*

Customer-service is a literal service to customers and all other stakeholders in the enterprise, and that, like architecture itself, it is an attitude that needs to pervade everything and be the personal responsibility of everyone across the overall shared-enterprise.

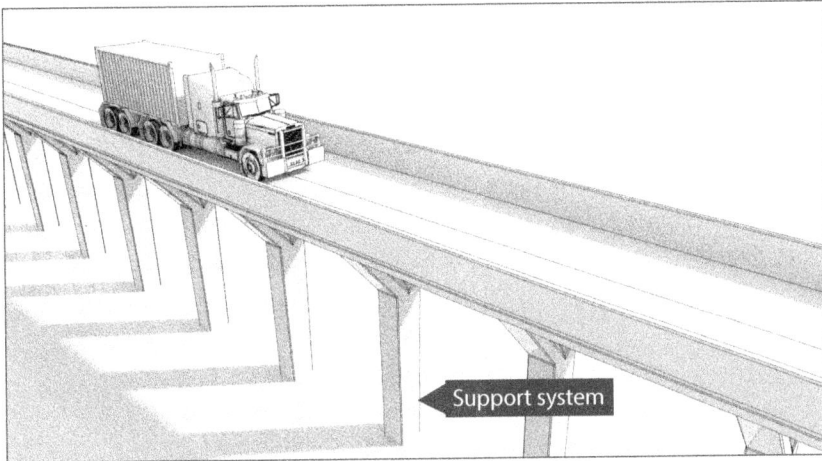

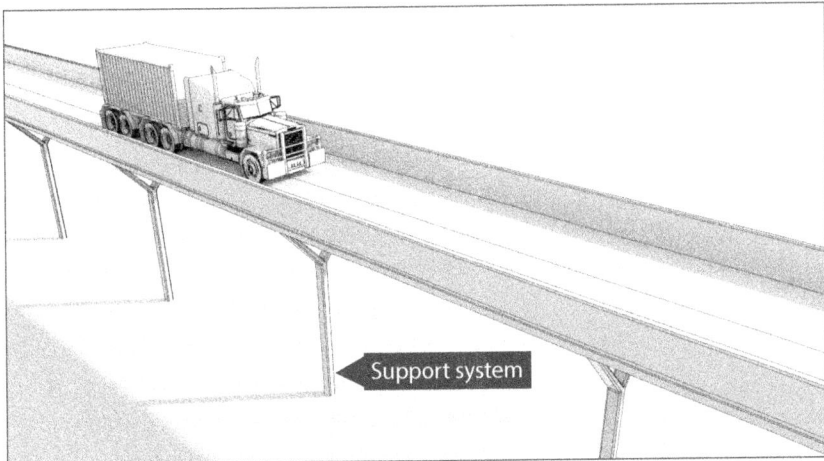

Contexts often require high levels of necessary-inefficiency in support-systems, and any attempts to trim below that level of necessary-inefficiency risks damaging overall effectiveness.

16: Architecture governance

What is the point of governance? What is its role in enterprise-architecture? Is it anything more than the dreaded *'architecture police'*, governance for governance's sake?

Governance should never be *'an end in itself'*. Instead, governance exists solely to support a business need or, more specifically, to keep things on track towards that business-need.

It is not as simple as a hierarchy, more like intersecting sets, some of which might seem from some viewpoints to seem to be in hierarchical relationships, but from other viewpoints are not hierarchical at all.
For example, regulatory and compliance constraints are routine drivers for governance that might apply directly only within one business-domain, but may well impact on *'higher'* business-needs.
An simplistic approach to governance, partitioned only according to a preconceived hierarchy, may seem to work well within the local context, but can cause serious whole-of-system problems elsewhere.

Next, what governance is really about, at the most general level, is the real *'Why?'* behind enterprise-architecture:
That things work better when they work together, on purpose.

It is crucial to be aware here that the *'things'* in question, for governance, are not only those to which the immediate governance might seem to apply. But how those *'things'* intersect with and impact on everything else within the overall enterprise: how those *'things'* support *purpose* as a whole.

So where does the *'business need'* come from?
There are two key points here. The first is that we actually need governance for all of these concerns, not only the governance of the implementation. *(Technically, we also need governance of governance itself)*
The second is that is that these needs are not so much in a hierarchy as something more like a network. Which is why we not only need a form of governance to match. This is where architecture comes into the picture, as the capability within the enterprise tasked with the theme of *'things work better when they work together, on purpose'*.
It is a mesh: our job is to prevent it collapsing into a mess…

The danger is that it is easy to think of this as entirely top-down. Big-picture strategic-intent, to change-roadmap, to detailed-plan, and then to implementation of each individual plan, with full traceability and control all the way back up to the original big-picture intent. An implementation of the grand top-down master-plan. The catch, of course, is that the real world has very different ideas about how the world works, especially in the kind of context of wildly-dynamic change such as we so often have to work with in real-world enterprise-architecture.

Which is where governance comes into the picture, but not as top-down 'control'. Not if we want it to succeed, anyway.

The main perspective we need to hold is that governance is not the Department of 'No', it's the Department of 'Yes-And...' It is not about 'control', it is about negotiation with the practicalities and demands of reality. Things change, contexts change, needs change, options change, constraints change, implementations change, and all of it is happening dynamically, all at the same time, across an entire architecture. If we think we have any real control over all of that, or can stop all of that change happening, we would be deluding ourselves, and others. Instead, we have to work with all of that change, whilst still holding to the initial intent. That is the real trick; that is what governance is really about, and really for.

And that is why we need all those descriptive tools and techniques such as architecture-principles, and enterprise-vision and values. They provide anchors or ultimate reference-points to guide decision-making. Especially for the more difficult and challenging decisions, where nothing else seems certain. That is why we need reference-frameworks, and that is why we need sense-making tools such as *SCAN (mentioned earlier)*, they help to guide decision-making when things get uncertain.

A practical example, from our work at Australia Post: three projects all wanting to use *RFID*[1] technologies, each incompatible with each other, all needing to operate in the same physical space, and one of which would require all of its data actually being owned by an external corporation. The point for governance is simply to point out that each of these is a governance-issue:
- *given the core theme of 'things work better when they work together', we really can't allow such a situation to develop with things that definitely can't work together*
- *we have an architectural principle, taken from a legal constraint that is binding on the corporation as a whole, that core enterprise-data must remain under the control and ownership of the corporation at all times*

Remember, that governance is the Department of 'Yes, and...' so *"Yes, this is what you each want to do, and yes, you each have valid reasons for wanting to do it this way; and this way isn't going to work across the whole; so let's sit down and work out another way that will work better, together"*.

As enterprise-architects, what we do not try to do here is tell solution-architects and system-designers how to do their job: if nothing else, they are likely to have a much better understanding of current technologies and their capabilities than we do, and we do need to show them respect. Instead, our role in this kind of governance is to quietly hold our ground in

---

1. RFID
RFID (Radio-frequency identification) uses electromagnetic fields to automatically identify and track tags attached to objects. Wikipedia

relation to the original plan, the roadmap, the business-need, the principles and the overall vision. Emphasising that each of these have their validity too, and should not be overridden casually just to make life a little bit easier in the short-term for individual designers and developers. As well, to guide conversations about how to do things better, about how to hold to that core theme of *'things work better when they work together, on purpose'.*

That dynamic network of purpose is what we most need to work with here. Everyone has their own purpose, their own intent, their own drivers, their own reasons for doing things, or wanting to do things, the way that they do. Our job is to acknowledge all of that, respect all of that, and hold people gently to the shared-purpose that underpins both the organisation and the larger shared-enterprise within which it operates.
Using project-plans, roadmaps, principles, values, vision and the like as guidelines for each of those governance-conversations.

Playing *the Department Of No*, with top-down *diktat*[1] and rigid enforcement, always looks like the easier way to do governance, and certainly is much more appealing to architects' egos. The catch, though, is that it just does not work well at all. All it does is breed annoyance, resistance, and *under-the-cover* short-term hacks that can be really disastrous in the larger scheme of things. Besides, the people on whom that kind of top-down *'governance'* is so often inflicted may instead be the only ones who are right. By contrast, respectful conversations via the *Department Of Yes-And* is what does work: and the outcomes of those explorations often open up great opportunities for the wider whole.

Ultimately that's what governance is all about: conversations, about purpose, and finding ever-better ways to keep to that purpose, in ways that work better for everyone and everything working together.

---

1. Diktat
A diktat is a harsh penalty or settlement imposed upon a defeated party by the victor. Wikipedia

---

17: The hard questions

"Never expect someone to get it if their income, job or status depend on not getting it". That's a challenge that enterprise-architects and others face every single day...

Within the enterprise, we are tasked with finding ways to implement and support the core theme of all architecture, *that things work better when they work together, on purpose.* Yet what can we do when:
• *We find some part within the enterprise that is blocking 'working together'*
• *People seem incapable of understanding what part it is, or what's needed to resolve it*
• *People already know that part doesn't work, but are either carefully ignoring it in the hope that it will magically solve itself, or are even intentionally maintaining that flaw for personal profit or gain?*

To give a concrete example, we now know, without any possible doubt, that *Taylorism[1]* only works well within a very small set of circumstances. In other words:
• *random numeric targets*
• *"our strategy is last year plus 10%"*
• *input-based metrics*
• *money-centric definitions of 'value'[2]*
• *rigid separation of analysis and action*
• *top-down control*
• *fragmentation via silo-based hierarchies*
• *parasitic 'owner'-relationships*

which lead to a *'management'*-centric concept of the organisation.

Waivers
So what can we do to reduce these issues, mentioned above? As architects, it is explicitly our professional and ethical duty to warn about the dangers of them. Yet often it is clear that no-one is listening, sometimes very pointedly *'not-listening',* too... And yet if we do continue to push on this, the only likely outcome will be a *'shoot-the-messenger'* exercise in which we get fired. Fortunately, there is a way out of this mess, the waiver.

---

1. Taylorism
Frederick Taylor in the 1880s explored using science to improve productivity in the workplace. Critics of his concepts felt that people became like cogs in machines, which might help an organisation at the expense of the workers.
2. Value
See Tools for Change-mapping, page 6, for more details about assessing value, using four aspects: Virtual, Physical, Relational and Aspirational.

Our role as enterprise-architects is mainly one of **decision-support**, not **decision-making.** We can, do and should give advice on architectural concerns, developed to the best of our ability, but unless we are explicitly asked to make decisions, the final decisions are not ours to make. And that distinction is crucial *(not least for our continued employment…).*

If we have done our job well, we should have a pretty clear idea of what would work in the enterprise, and what won't. What will support *'things-working-together'* and what won't. Our advice should indicate and describe that overall understanding, in terms appropriate for that audience.
Our advice should mean something, the kind of advice which is unwise to ignore, especially at the scope and scale of an enterprise-architecture.
So if our advice is then dismissed or ignored, we do need to make it clear to all involved that there are likely to be consequences for the organisation and its business, consequences that could well cause serious damage. It is that that we need to document in a waiver.

In effect, rejection of enterprise-architecture advice would usually represent a conscious and intentional decision on someone's part to create a non-conformance to the architecture, which, by definition, represents a verifiable architectural risk. Sometimes such risks are necessary and unavoidable: for example, in classic IT-oriented architecture, that some system or functionality that we need is simply not available at the current time. But whenever such risks are created, we must review them at some future date, and take action to reduce them as soon as possible.

A waiver should include at least the following items:
• *the context of the architectural-advice (such as the initial business-question, and the respective scope within the overall enterprise-architecture)*
• *the advice that was given (the architectural response to the business-question)*
• *the expected consequences of compliance and of non-compliance to that advice (opportunities and benefits, and risks, both direct and indirect)*
• *the basis for that advice (frameworks, assumptions and so on, in part to reduce our own tendencies towards 'policy-based evidence'[1])*
• *supporting-materials for the advice (presentation slide-decks, architectural-models, assessment-materials, etc)*
• *identifiers for the presenter of each part of that advice (indicating that the advice was given)*
• *identifiers for the decision-maker for each part of that advice (indicating accountability for the decision)*
• *the decision taken by the decision-makers (indicating the risks and consequences for which each decision-maker has now accepted personal responsibility and accountability, against the architects' advice)*

---

1. Policy-based evidence
See Whole Enterprise Architecture, page 109, for more policy-based evidence.

The last item is crucially important for us as architects, because it may well provide necessary evidence for defence for the architect if *(or, more likely, when)* everything goes wrong as a result of the decision-makers' choice to reject architects' advice.

One more essential item for a waiver:
• *the review-date and/or event-triggers at which the waiver must be reassessed and reviewed*

This too is crucially-important, because if we don't include triggers for an explicit review-process, the waiver will simply become quietly forgotten and then, in all probability, conveniently *'lost'* when things do later go wrong. CEOs and other executives move on; even the most useless of managers eventually move on. Hype-bandwagons eventually fade; and whenever that happens, opportunities may arise to review past errors, and repair the damage that may or will have been done by poor architectural decisions. That is when waivers really prove their value.

One aspect of architecture where we are likely to need to create and monitor a lot of waivers is around service-oriented architectures at whole-enterprise scale, services in the most general sense, not just IT-services. The reason for this is that alongside the known-problematic services are likely to be some very serious service design-flaws, or what I describe as *disservices*. And, rather like the Taylorism example above, many of those arise from causes that many people would very much prefer not to be noticed or known, regardless of how much damage the resulting flaws do to the enterprise. As architects, we need waivers, and systematic processes to support them, as a means to give us at least some relative safety as we work with those issues.

Critics of Taylorism felt that people became like cogs in machines.

⬠⬠⬠⬠⬠ *Taken from the chapter:* **Professionalism, waivers and the hard questions**

18: Business motivation

What is the source of business-motivation? How are people motivated to do their work at work? The answer isn't much to do with money, at least, not for anything more than the most robotic kinds of work. Instead, the real drivers that matter most in business are **autonomy, mastery** and **purpose**.

Autonomy is about choosing our path through the work, being self-directed.
Mastery is about developing and using our skills, pushing ourselves to create ever-better work.
Purpose is about work that is meaningful in some way, that creates a sense of achieving or contributing towards some distinct aim or goal.

In practice it is simplest to think of motivation as the human gas-pedal: it is not the fuel or energy, but the motivation is what makes the energy available to do the work that's desired.

How can we help people maintain, or better, that level of motivation at work? Which is where we hit up against the business-motivation dilemma: *The more the organisation tries to control what and how things are done,* **the less motivation there will be to do the work that the organisation wants done.**

The first thing we ask people to do in a business is to give up some of their autonomy, in order to work as part of a team or the company.

The next thing we do is that we are likely to ask them to follow procedures, reducing the skill and the challenge. And we are also going to ask them to work towards the collective purpose rather than their own purpose.

So unless we do something to counter these natural impacts on motivation, the very fact of bringing someone into a company will automatically reduce their motivation to do the work of the company.
As above, if we are not careful, the motivation will go negative, leading to *'presenteeism'*: the person is present, and costing the organisation money and more, but not much in the form of constructive work is actually being done, in effect, negative motivation leading to negative performance. Negative-motivation in one person will also tend to pull others' motivation down too, towards a dysfunctional mess.

The conventional business answer is that we offer them money instead, as *'compensation'* for loss of autonomy, mastery and purpose. Yet money doesn't work well as a motivator for knowledge-work, giving people more money actually sends the quality of work down, not up.

Yet if money won't work, then what do we do? What business-architectures will preserve and enhance business-motivation for the people who work in that business? We can boost autonomy by ensuring that at least some of the work is self-directed, or in teams that are self-directed. And we can reduce the risk of further de-motivation by removing micromanagement and similar problems from the context.

We can boost mastery by ensuring that the work includes personal challenge and personal skills-development. And we can reduce the risk of further de-motivation by carefully putting into context, any Taylorist-style *'business process reengineering'*.

We can boost purpose by ensuring clear links between personal goals and collective goals, creating emotive reasons for personal commitment towards those shared aims. And we can reduce the risk of further de-motivation, by refocussing organisational attention on the shared-enterprise rather than on the divergent goals of shareholders and other *'non-enterprise'* stakeholders.

The more that any one of those drivers slumps down, the more we will need to lift the others up, just to keep the same level of effective motivation. If the context can't allow anything more than a near-zero autonomy, we can perhaps compensate if we boost either mastery or purpose far enough to become an intense personal driver. And if the motivation goes too far down on more than one strand, there is no way that we boost the remaining driver high enough to make it work. For almost every organisation, there is a delicate trade-off to manage here, and it is not as easy as it looks…
It is also not as simple as I have summarised it here: the relationships between those drivers is more likely to be a complex cross-leverage than a straightforward addition. But if we want to avoid the motivation-dilemma, we need to keep track of all of those strands, autonomy, mastery, purpose, and money too. And ensure that our architectures do support them as best we can, to create and maintain the motivation that will be needed throughout the organisation if it is to be able to achieve its aims.

The drivers that matter most in business are autonomy, mastery and purpose.

⬠⬠⬠⬠⬠ *Taken from the chapter:* **The motivation dilemma**

19: Continuous-improvement

Continuous-improvement is the cornerstone of many recent innovations in the business world. The mantra of *"release early, release often"* has been a factor in the success of many Open Source software projects. There are many other important advantages to continuous change: improvements take effect much quicker, feedback-cycles are faster, there is better engagement on the shop-floor, and so on. When applied well, such improvements echo all the way down to a much-improved bottom-line.

Yet though we may need to think sideways to spot it, there is also one important catch to continuous-change. Continuous improvement depends on large numbers of small incremental changes; the smaller the change, the faster that all-important feedback/improvement cycle can run. But in perceptual psychology, small changes are invisible, a change has to be of significant size before it becomes noticeable. In a well designed continuous-improvement process, often the whole point is that each change should be almost invisible, because it can reduce the stress of change, and allows potentially-challenging changes to be introduced by respectful *'stealth'* rather than in a single overwhelming *'big-bang'.* But the more that the improvement process succeeds in that task, the less anyone will notice each change. Which means that the change-team may appear to be doing no work at all. Which is not a good career-move…

Worse, if no-one notices the change, and no-one seems to notice it, then perceptions of product or service may be stuck at first impressions, which may be long out of date. Sometimes the classic *'big-bang'* Waterfall-style projects seem successful because their long release-cycles mean that the step-change introduced with each new release is large enough to be noticed.

Some proprietary projects look better because they use a less-effective change-process. Not exactly a desirable outcome…

Part of this is marketing, of course: a big step-change gives a good excuse for an *'event'* that's much more noticeable than a quiet, continuous, stolid, *'steady as she goes'.* Yet that is a tactic that's worth adopting in continuous-improvement processes: invent an *'event'* of your own, to celebrate change and advertise the improvements that have been implemented since the last *'event'.* That way you will make the work more noticeable, and more valued.

There is a subtle trade-off here. You will want every change to be noticed, but if you set the spacing of *'events'* too close together, not only will the events blur together too much to be noticeable, but you actually run the risk of increasing people's *'change-fatigue'.*

A common practice in open-source software-development is set to formal *'release-events'* at six-monthly or yearly intervals, even though there will often be many *'point-releases'* in the intervening period. Another useful tactic there is to use names rather than numbers to designate each major change.

Some typical themes in a *'release-event'* might include:
- *Summary of key groups of change, keep this list short, no more than 5-7 items*
- *Acknowledgement of key people involved in inventing or implementing significant changes*
- *Linking process-enhancements to key performance indicators at the whole-of-enterprise level*
- *Celebration of the value of change itself*

Keep each change and each change-cycle small enough to enhance improve effectiveness every day; yet also ensure that overall change is large enough to be visible and valued. That is the balance we aim to achieve here.

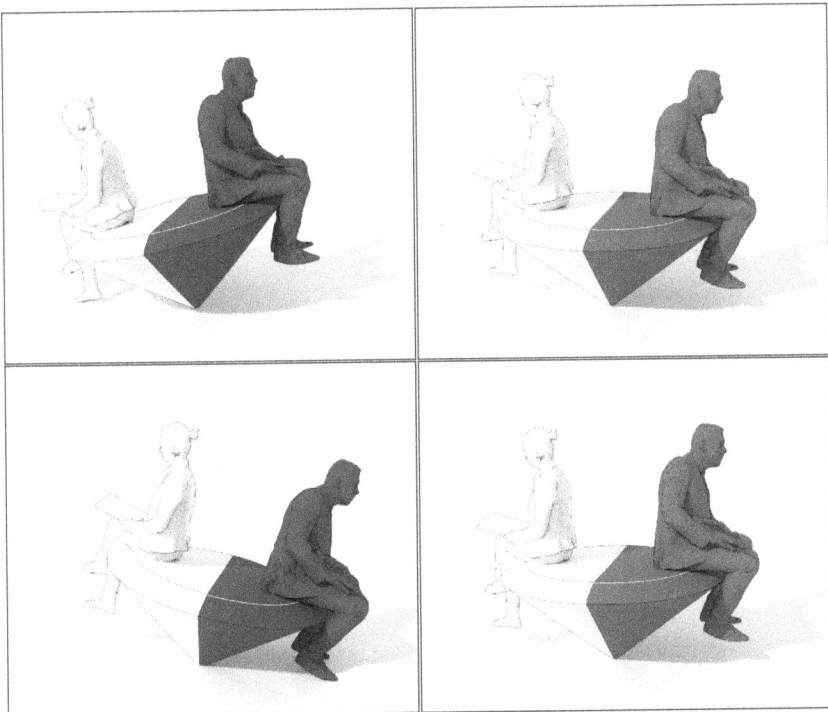

Try to balance between small cycle-change to improve effectiveness and change that is large enough to be visible and valued.

⬠⬠⬠⬠⬠ *Taken from the chapter: **Making continuous-improvement visible***

20: Why before who

Does the customer always come first? Do customer-needs drive everything? For that matter, is the customer always right?

If we do get these wrong, in our strategy, our business-model, our customer-journey mapping or whatever, we set ourselves up for a failure that will be worse because on the surface it seems so much *'the right thing to do'*…

There is a really simple way to reframe this, but it needs a bit of explanation first.

In this simple example, the person represents a service moving from the real world (realised ends) towards the vision (desired ends). The person is the means to travel towards the vision.

To start with, let's take *'the reason why anything happens'*:
Why anything happens is that there's a tension between what we want *(the desired-ends, 'the vision')* versus what we have *(the realised-ends, 'the real-world')*. Somewhere along that tension, we decide to do something *(the means, 'the service')* to reach towards those desired-ends.

To put it another way, the tension between vision and the real-world provides the *'Why'* for the service.

Out of that *'Why'* also fall various values and principles and more that determine the meaning of *'success'* for that service.

The values and principles provide metrics and guidance that help us to determine whether our service is more, or less, on-track towards its vision, its desired-ends.

In most cases, we share some aspects of that service with others, most visibly in the form of service-provision *from* others *('suppliers')*, and service-provision *to* others *('customers')*, a value-flow:

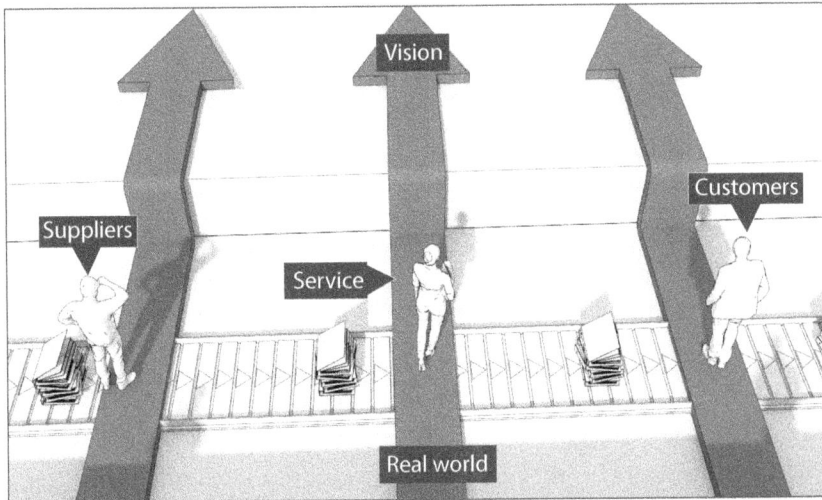

A simple example of a value flow. The service requires supplies from the suppliers, which it passes on to its customers.

This gives us the classic *'business-model'* relationships. Which can be expanded out indefinitely in both directions into a value-web or, more simply, a linear supply-chain of transactions, where we have the supplier's suppliers and the customer's customers.

Yet if we focus only on this horizontal flow of transactions, it is easy to miss something really important: there is no **'Why'** shown there, other than the unexpressed **'Why'** that arises from **Who**, **How** and **What**.

This is exactly the reason why so many people misunderstand the nature and role of *'value-proposition',* describing it as *"the fancy name for your product or service"*. It is not: instead, the value-proposition is how we propose to deliver value, first in terms of the vision *(the Why)*. And then in terms of the value-flow between the parties in those transactions *(the How and With-What)*. We also need to note that the real context of the business-model is much broader than that overly-simplistic single step supply-chain from supplier to self to customer.

A typical view of a value flow. Suppliers supply organisations, who supply customers.

In reality, we need to expand our awareness from the example shown above to more like the example shown below.

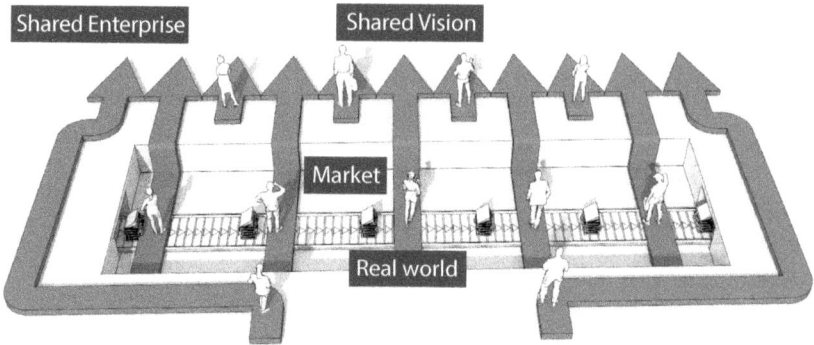

A more complete view of the shared enterprise. In the centre is the market, all supplying or being supplied goods or services. In the area above are stakeholders. while not part of the market are part of the shared enterprise, whether they want to be or not. In the shared enterprise we see top left to right: community, government, anti-clients (people dissatisfied with organisation) and various others. Along the bottom: investors and beneficiaries of the shared enterprise. The grey arrows show the shared vision for the enterprise

And for which the enterprise-vision, the shared **Why** for all stakeholders in that overall service-context, provides the reason why those stakeholders connect *(even if only briefly)* with each other.

The **Who** of the customer does come before the **How** and **What** of our business-model and we do need to ensure that the customer is satisfied before the service-cycle as a whole can be considered complete.

Yet it also shows us that *'completion for customer'* is not the end of the cycle It is not just about satisfying the customer. Instead, it's about *'completion for all'*, providing satisfaction for all stakeholders, including those who are *'in the story'* even though they may not interact much with us directly, if at all.

What this really tells us is that, whatever we do, and whoever we do it with, we need to satisfy the shared-**Why** as much, if not more, than the **Who**, **How** and **With-What**.

This also suggests another useful cross-map about the focus within each of the stages of the service-cycle:
• *Why: shared-enterprise*
• *Who: strategy*
• *How: tactics*
• *What and With-What: operations*

Which, in turn, highlights another crucial concern for the business-model: the **Why**, and its connected values and principles, provide a means to distinguish between *'good'* and *'bad'* customers *(and suppliers, too).*

'Good' customers, suppliers and others align themselves with the same enterprise-vision, values and principles; *'bad'* ones don't, and instead are just along for the ride or for what they can take. We can maybe satisfy a *'bad'* customer, but in doing so we fail the test for *'completion for all'*, which breaks the cycle of expanding and continually-reaffirming the shared-trust and shared-commitments upon which the overall shared-enterprise will depend. To make it work, and work well for everyone in the shared enterprise-story, we need to use the shared-story's vision, values and principles to show us how, where and when to engage, and when not to engage, with any alleged player in that story.

That is why that shared-**Why** is so important: keeping on-track towards it reduces the risk of waste in any form, whether in terms of effort *('completion of the right task')*, profit *('completion for self')*, satisfied transactors *('completion for customer/supplier')* and the shared-enterprise as a whole *('completion for all stakeholders')*.
Which brings us to that *"simpler way to frame this"* that I promised back at the start of this explanation: that **Why** comes before **Who**.
Which tells us that the customer doesn't come first: the shared-story does. And which also tells us that the customer is not always right: at times they may well be wrong, in terms of that story. *(Not 'wrong' in any supposed-'absolute' sense, but simply in context of that story.)*

21: Employees as customers of HR

What is the proper, or most effective, relationship between the
'Human Resources' department and the employees of an organisation?

Recently I was running an EA-related workshop for the HR management of a
mid-sized multinational conglomerate, a pleasant change from the usual IT-
only enterprise-architecture! Many of their concerns are much the same as
for IT: they worry about *'HR-business alignment',* they want HR to been seen
as strategic and deserving of a place at the executive table and so on.
And yet just as with IT, most of what they do seems stuck in transactions. It's
different from IT, yet also much the same.
Of the stream of ideas and tactics that have come up in these sessions,
perhaps the most interesting is this: employees are the customers of HR.

Think of that relationship exactly the same as in any other business-model:
in effect, HR is *'selling'* employment in the company to potential and current
employees. If HR is a service-provider for the business, employees are its
active customers, in a straightforward multi-sided business-model.
The shocking part, though, is that if the business treated its *'outside'*
customers in the way that HR treats the employees, the business probably
wouldn't have a business at all…
To make sense of this, and also to help HR to find its desired role as a partner
in business-strategy, then probably our best approach is to map HR and its
processes onto a frame of inside-in, inside-out, outside-in and outside-out.

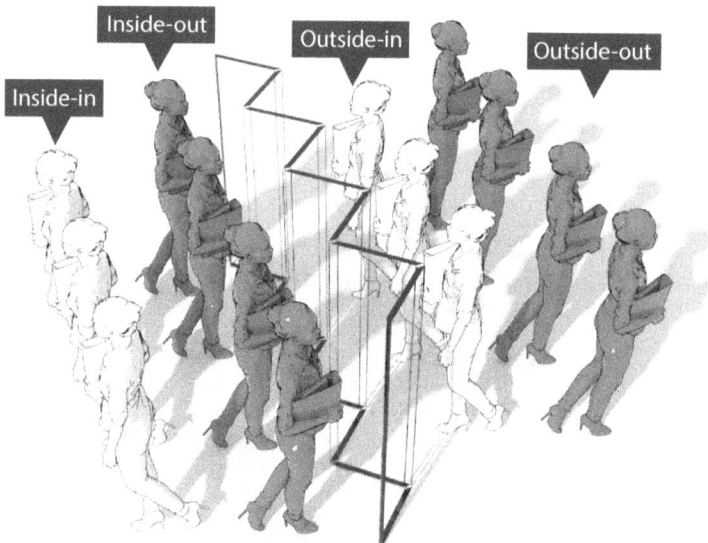

Four types of perspectives of HR (see overleaf for details).

The transaction aspect is **'inside-in'**, making sure that the HR processes are efficient and reliable and so on, solely from the perspective of the systems themselves. As with most IT-architecture work, it doesn't take long before we realise that even from that perspective the current systems can be a long way from what they could be, with all manner of legacy issues and local-optimisations and so on, that will need cleaning up on an ongoing basis.

Much of HR's relationship with everyone else, perhaps especially in that long-established staple of the HR world, the 'job-description', is classic **'inside-out'**: the world viewed only from our own perspective. We have a job that needs doing, here's the description of the the requirements for that task, who can we find to fill that gap?

And it's much the same as in classic 'push-marketing': here's the 'value-proposition', here are the features, here's the price, come and get it. It's sort-of the other way round to sales, buying services, rather than selling them, but that's almost the only difference.

The catch is that, on its own, **'inside-out'** doesn't work well. For example, in one part of the business, there's a huge turnover of employees: the 'value' part of the employment value-proposition, it seems, can wear away very fast indeed. Which can lead to huge costs of acquisition, retention and de-acquisition, even in financial terms, let alone human ones.

What is missing is those other two perspectives, **'outside-in'**, and **'outside-out'**. In our example, **'outside-in'** means looking at things from the employee's perspective. Asking *"Why would anyone want to work for you, or with you?"* If the only reason on offer is money, don't expect good results. Instead, think of it exactly the same as for any other customer-journey: what are the touch-points, the areas of friction, of satisfaction and dissatisfaction? Viewing an employee as a customer in this sense can often be a real eye-opener, leading to a literally revolutionary shift in how the organisation engages with *(emphasis: 'with')* its employees. As revolutionary as 'pull-marketing' is in the organisation's relationships with its customers.

And to make that 'pull' possible, to make it work, we also need an **'outside-out'** perspective: viewing the shared-enterprise in its own terms, broader than the scope of our own organisation or any other. **'Outside-out'** is about shared-purpose, the 'vision' or unifying-theme and connected values that link everyone together in that shared-enterprise, and that provide the deeper reason why people want to engage with each other in that context.

In employment, the classic example is the old story of a janitor sweeping the floors in a NASA office in the late 1960s: when asked what he was doing, he answered *"I'm helping to put a man on the Moon"*.

Given a purpose that means something to them, most people will want to work, in almost whatever way they can; but without that purpose, they won't, sometimes even regardless of how much they are paid.

Just as with any customer, an employee needs a reason to engage with the organisation's own purpose: an *'outside-out'* view of the shared-enterprise will help us to identify what that purpose is.

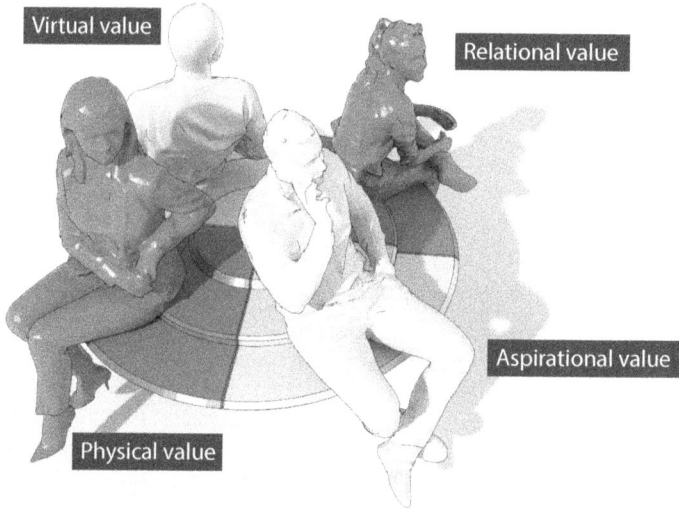

For each part of the Inside-out tool we can also look in more detail at what is valued. For example Outside-in (what the enterprise values), can be split into four aspects, as shown above. If we imagine what employees of an airport might value in terms of:

Virtual value. Having clear, up to date information about work schedules.
Physical value. That the airport provides a safe working environment.
Relational value. Work issues can be easily discussed with management.
Aspirational. There is a clear sense of purpose about everything we do.

Part 2:

Business architecture challenges

This section of the book is an abridged version of
Business architecture challenges'
www.leanpub.com/tp-bizchallenge

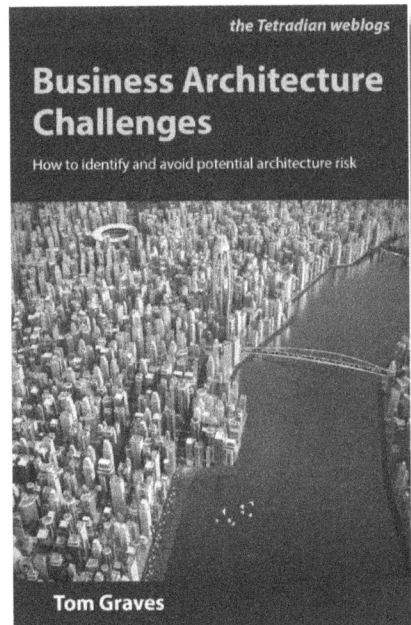

the Tetradian weblogs

Business Architecture Challenges

How to identify and avoid potential architecture risk

Tom Graves

22: The architecture of management

Why is management the way that it is? Does it work well that way? And what part does the architecture of management play in determining how well it does or doesn't work?

I have repeatedly come across four seemingly clear themes:
- *a deeper exploration of the architectural idea that everything in the enterprise is or represents a service*
- *watching architecture colleagues in several different organisations struggle with ridiculous demands from management-hierarchies that do not work*
- *deeper exploration of conceptual flaws in current economics, particularly around the concept of possession and 'rights of possession'*
- *watching yet deeper cracks appear in the current worldwide economic system*

For me there's been a kind of nagging suspicion that there might be some strong inter-relationships across all of that conceptual space. Which in turn leads me to several deeply-worrying questions, from an architectural perspective, if nothing else:
- *If everything is a service, what services, if any, does management actually deliver to the enterprise?*
- *If everything is a service, why should management be assigned any priority over anything else?*
- *Why are management-services and management overall so consistently inefficient and ineffective?*
- *What part does organisational-structure play in making management-services so ineffective in practice?*
- *Why is it assumed that 'promoting' someone into management will necessarily improve overall service-delivery?*
- *Why is it so often assumed that the most effective way of organising management-services is a top-down hierarchy of supposed 'control' of all other services?*
- *Following the trails of prioritised service-relationships, why are financial-shareholders so often assigned priority over every other service*
- *In the current socio-political context, what can we do architecturally to make any of this work any better?*

Let's explore a bit more about each of those questions above.

If everything is a service, what services does management nominally deliver to the enterprise?

In *Enterprise Canvas*[1], the services typically delivered by *'the management'* are described as *'direction services'*, with three distinct components:

---

1. Enterprise Canvas
See Tools for Change-mapping, page 18 for an overview of a simple version of this tool.

- *'develop the business', identify organisational and enterprise vision,
  and keep the organisation on-track to vision*
- *'change the business', explore external (and internal) context, to identify
  required strategic change*
- *'run the business', use tactical and operational information to assess activity,
  allocate resources and guide decision-making*

Following classic military organisational models, management-services are often split between *'staff'* and *'line'.* This split can be interpreted as follows:
- *'staff level management', group information and decision-making in terms
  of the big picture*
- *'line management' tend to focus at what is happening the front line*

In a Taylorist model of management, services that should function at right angles to the *'direction-services'* are often inappropriately bundled under the *'management'* domain. These include:
- *coordination-services, coordination of planning for overall change, detailed
  management of change, and run-time coordination of
  inter-service transactions*
- *validation-services, developing awareness and capability to keep on track
  to values, and performance in relation to those values*

Broadly, in classic Taylorism, anything that is not specifically about production or service-delivery, and could be seen as in some way related to *'control'* of others, is placed under the exclusive scope and privilege of *'management'.* Taylorism places a strict boundary between *'management'* and *'workers'.* Yet from a service-architecture perspective, management itself is another form of service-delivery, the delivery of *'management-services',* it is not viewed as structurally different from anything else.

If everything is a service, why should management be assigned any priority over anything else?

There is no valid reason at all, from a services-perspective. It is just another service, or set of services.

The only possible reason why management might be assigned random priority over other services is from mistaken assumptions about *'rights of control'.* For the most part, these assumptions come from an unfortunate coincidence of functions within the *'management-services':*
- *services for strategic-assessment, potentially giving the mistaken idea that
  'knowing more about big-picture' means 'responsibility to' tell others what
  to do'*
- *services for coordination of resource-allocation, potentially giving the a
  mistaken assumption of authority over others via 'right to withhold'.
  This comes from a mistaken idea about the dysfunctional role of imagined
  'rights of possession' within the broader society, and so within an
  organisation's economic model.*

Architecturally speaking, this is not a defensible reason for priority. Every service is *'just another service'* that is required for enterprise viability, so no service can be said to have automatic priority over any other.

Why are management-services and management overall so inefficient and ineffective?

The main reason is failure to understand that management-services are *'just another service',* without any automatic priority over any other.

The assumption of priority feeds a mistaken idea of *'right'* to regard and treat others as either *'object'* or *'subject'* of that person. For obvious reasons, this rarely works well in a social context…

What part does organisational-structure play in making management-services so ineffective in practice?

Probably a lot, though it's often far from obvious as to exactly how and why this should be.

Two themes do come to mind. One is that the Taylorist split between *'management'* and *'workers'* means that anything *'not-work'* is pushed into the 'management' space. *(This is another variant of the same driver that creates IT-centrism or business-centrism, but in reverse.)*
A key side-effect of this is that the non-run-time coordination-services and virtually all of the validation-services are included under the *'management'* banner, where they most definitely do not belong. As the Viable System Model makes clear, these categories of services are necessarily at right-angles to the direction-services (*'management'*). If these services are grouped into *'management',* the automatic result, as shown in every *'control'*-oriented organisation, will be the creation of covert *'shadow-networks'* in order to get actual work done. This inevitably creates inefficiencies, misalignment, miscommunication, and many conflicts with *'the management'* .

The other theme arises from the Victorian *(and so Taylorist)* passion for hierarchies of *'control'.* A tree-structure works well as a means to collect information and develop abstractions and overviews. And also as a means to distribute guidance-information *(and resources in general)* from a central point. However, a tree-structure is not good for coordinating end-to-end business-processes, because it forces all cross-silo coordination up towards the *'top'* of the tree, creating serious bottlenecks for flows.

And as *Deming*[1] showed, it's also often a very poor structure for decision-making and control, because of the *'Taylorist trap'*: the skill-sets and abilities needed to solve concrete front-line problems become less and less available the further *'upward',* more-abstract, that we move in the hierarchy-tree.

There are probably many other examples of how management-structures impact effectiveness: there's a lot more exploration needed here. These two themes are destructive enough already, though...

Why is it assumed that *'promoting'* someone into management will improve overall service-delivery?

We could suggest that it is the historical result of three related yet distinct strands:

Possession-based economics gave rise to the idea of personal 'rights' to collective resources.

Capitalism provided the view that 'the owners' had exclusive 'rights' to organisational resources, and therefore had exclusive say in how those resources were distributed and used.

Feudalism[2] supported the view of 'superiority' and 'inferiority', and the so called 'right' of 'superiors' to determine and demand the actions of their 'inferiors'.

The result is a peculiar tree-type structure that can work well for specific functions in certain specific contexts. In all too many cases, though, it tends to collapse into a dysfunctional mess.

In possessionist capitalism, *'rights'* to organisational resources are directly related to 'position' on the tree-of-control. *'Promotion' (and its counterpart 'demotion')* is a re-positioning on that tree, and so an amendment of *'rights to resources',* both organisational resources and, via *'remuneration',* to the resources of society.

To put it in another way, *'promotion'* is the main mechanism within the current employment-based model via which competent people get more recognition and more *'stuff'.* Because the tree of-control is associated almost exclusively with the management-services, this often means that the only available means of enhanced recognition and remuneration is via *'promotion'* into the management-structure.

In principle, a management role implies increased responsibility to guide others: in a service-oriented enterprise, that is the real purpose for the management-services, and when that is the purpose for a *'promotion'* into management, it does work well. The problem is that the *'management=promotion'* assumes both that the person both wants to do that type of work with that increased responsibility for others, and is

---

1. Deming
William E. Deming is also known as the father of the quality movement and was credited with revolutionizing Japan's industry and making it one of the most dominant economies in the world. Wikipedia

2. Feudalism
*In the middle ages most people in Europe lived on lands 'owned' by lords.
In order to live on these lands they had to pay for the privilege, as well as honouring and fighting for the lords. The rich get richer and the poor get poorer.*

competent to do it anyway. Yet if the only means of increased recognition or resources is *'promotion'* into management, then that's what they will do, and sometimes they have no choice about it anyway.

The result is often serious damage to organisational effectiveness. The other side of the *'promotion'* is that someone who is usually very skilled at some other type of service-delivery is no longer available to do that work any more. To make it worse, becoming out of touch with front-line service-delivery may result in a steady erosion of their original competence, yet they may still believe that they know as much, if not more, than those who are currently doing front-line delivery. Courtesy of Taylorist theories about the nature of organisations, they may even believe that they automatically know more than others because they have been *'promoted'* to a management role.

Why is it assumed that the most effective way of organising management-services is a top-down hierarchy of 'control'?

Most of this comes from Taylorist and pre-Taylorist belief-systems, as summarised above.

The problem is two-fold. One part is that a tree-structure is a good way to cluster and abstract from performance-information, and to distribute directions within any context where centralised decision-making makes sense. There is therefore a tendency to assume that it will therefore work well in all contexts, which is not the case.
Top down hierarchy tends to succeed if:
• *the work is repetitive*
• *the work has simple rules*
• *the work has a cluster of control.*
• *performance-information can be handled by a simple tree-structure without 'top-of-tree' inter-silo bottlenecks,*
• *the context is not undergoing rapid change*

Top down hierarchy tends to fail if:
• *the work is knowledge-based or relationship-based*
• *localised decision-making is required*
• *any kind of communication is required*
• *the context is undergoing rapid change*

If so an alternative structure for management-services within that context must be used.

The other part of this is a hang-over from feudal times, where authority, responsibilities and *'rights'* were defined in terms of strict rules. A duke had the responsibility to lead an army, but was also responsible to raise the funds and everything else that the army would need; a count was responsible for taxation within a region, which often meant the need for a small army to enforce that taxation; and so on. A feudal model defines that all people *'below'* in the tree-of-control are subjects, literally, subject to the will of the *'superior'*, or acting as extensions of the *'superior's* will.

Psychologically speaking, it is a very interesting *'racket'*, because it enables all parties to claim the *'rights'* to any rewards but also the *'right'* to avoid responsibility for the consequences. The *'superior'* orders the action, but can avoid responsibility because only the *'inferiors'* actually did the action; the *'inferiors'* did the action, but can claim that they weren't responsible because they were *'only following orders'* from the *'superior'*.

It is the result of a classic logic-error, assuming that because something did work in one context, it must therefore continue to do so in that context and all other contexts. Architecturally speaking, we need to challenge this assumption in every case, because the consequences to the organisation's effectiveness are not good.

Why are financial-shareholders so often assigned priority over every service?
Really there is no defensible reason.

Financial shareholders are merely one category of investors in the organisation and enterprise: in almost all organisations and enterprises, there are many other types of investment than money, and many other categories of investor. Financial-shareholders are also often some of the least-responsible investors, given that the shareholding may now last mere milliseconds in some cases, and that shareholding in limited-liability companies involves quite considerable *'rights'* with almost zero responsibilities other than risk of loss of financial investment. Structurally, this represents a very high risk to the enterprise.

So called *'rights of possession'* only on the basis of financial investment, are rooted in an early-18th-century model of capitalism that is hopelessly out-of-date relative to the present-day business-context. For example, given that the core capital of many current organisations resides primarily in the minds and relationships of individual employees, the shareholder-model is often practically a declaration of *'right of possession'* of those individuals themselves. Again, huge structural problems here, for business-architecture especially, with a real risk that some of these structural flaws are already moving towards a point of catastrophic failure.

What can we do architecturally to make any of this work any better?
All of these are architectural problems, all with very severe consequences, and should concern those involved in all aspects of enterprise-architecture and its various domain-architectures.

However, in most cases they arise from very deep political roots, which can be complex to deal with.

The key here is to remember that, especially at this level, the architect's role is primarily one of decision-support, not decision-making. In most of these cases, the decisions belong to senior executives, boards and, further out, regulators and politicians and the like.

What we can do, and should do, is to gather the evidence that others will need in order to make those decisions. In many cases we also could develop and document preliminary options, including documenting the implications and social and other costs and consequences, so that those others can make informed decisions. That is our task here: attempting to do anything more than that will probably help no-one, and may cause a lot more harm than good, especially to us.

Probably the simplest way to deal with this, in an architectural sense, is to class all of the problems described above as breaches of valid architectural principles that have been allowed to go ahead anyway because of some overriding reason. In most cases, we can document the reason for the breach as *'political'.* Because all unresolved architectural breaches should be subject to regular review, eventually someone will have the courage to tackle these problems, and we can then at last take action to resolve them. But until then, we can at least ensure that they are not placed into the dreaded *'too hard basket',* where too many important problems lie indefinitely without attention until they have already gone past the point of no-return.

Some organisations have strange tree-like organisational structures.

⬠⬠⬠⬠⬠ *Taken from the chapter: **Rethinking the architecture of management***

23: Managers and leaders

Many organisations talk about *'developing new leaders'.* What they mostly mean in practice is *'developing new managers'.* Which is unfortunate, because they are not the same…

Many organisations have a surplus of managers, but a desperate shortage of leaders. To which the organisation responds by creating yet more managers, who believe themselves to be *'leaders'* because they are managers.
The core difference is right there in the job-description: **leaders lead, while managers manage.**

What managers manage are resources of various kinds: things, time and budgets, for example. Managers have an unfortunate tendency to regard everything as *'resources',* including people…

Managing resources is an important service to provide to a work-team or whatever. And when we map manager-roles onto the Five Element cycle, what we find is that managers sit as an add-on to the actual work of each phase, as shown below:

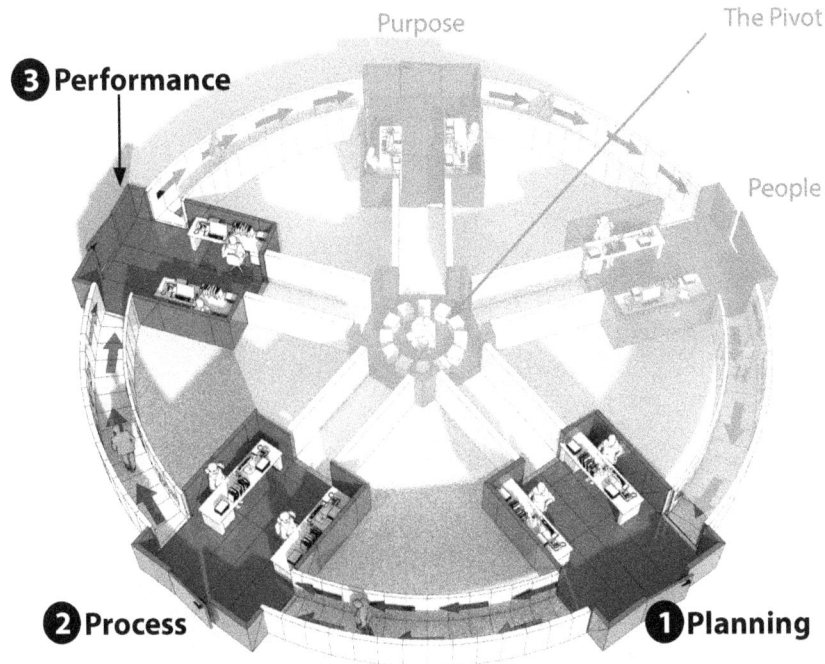

A simplified version of the Five Elements tool, showing manager's roles.
❶ *Manager for how resources will be used.*
❷ *Manager for how resources are being used.*
❸ *Manager for how resources were used.*

Managers keep things predictable, safe, certain. That is their main task, and many are very good at it.

Which would be fine, if the real-world actually worked that way.
Which, these days, it increasingly doesn't.

By contrast, leaders lead. We need leaders to guide the process of change, at every scale, from the smallest *(a single step in a business-process)* to the largest *(the purpose and strategy of the enterprise as a whole)*. And sometimes beyond even that.

We need leaders within every phase of the Five Element cycle, to guide the action when we focus on the Pivot, Purpose, People, Preparation, Process or Performance:

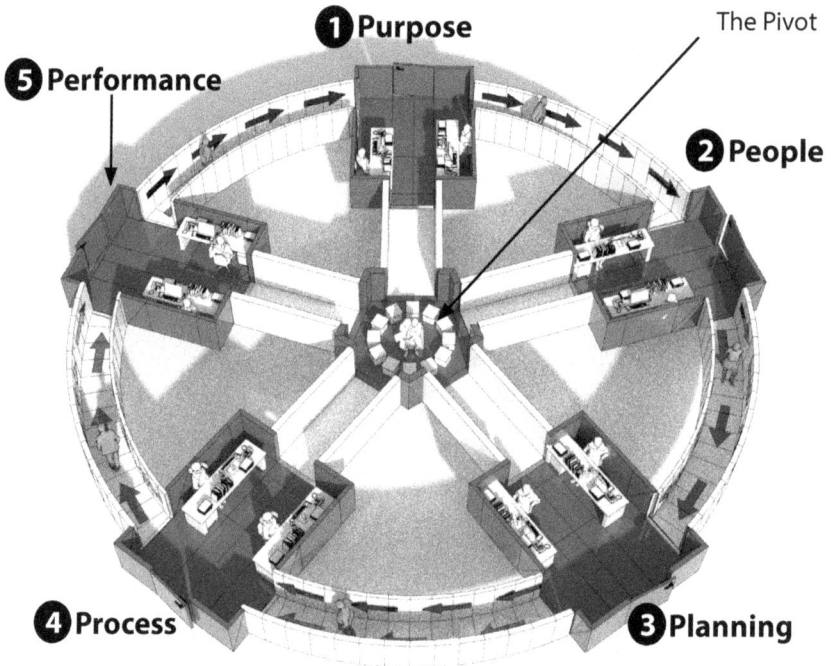

A simplified version of the Five Elements tool, showing Leader's roles.
1 *Leader for Purpose (Why we are doing the work).*
2 *Leader for People (Who we need to do the work).*
3 *Leader for Planning (What we need to do, to do the work).*
4 *Leader for Process (Doing the work).*
5 *Leader for Performance (Did we do the work well?).*
The Pivot acts as a hub for all the other roles (or rooms).

We need leaders between each of the Five Element phases, to guide as to when to stop working on the activities of one phase, and move on to the next:

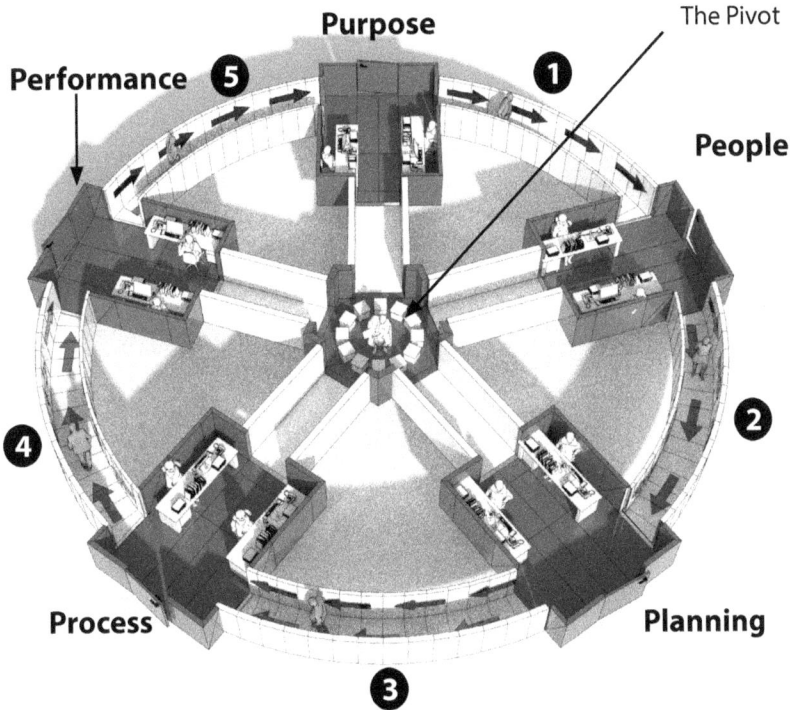

A simplified version of the Five Elements tool, showing Leader's roles.
1 Leader between Purpose/People
2 Leader between People/Planning
3 Leader between Planning/Process
4 Leader between Process/Performance
5 Leader between Performance/Purpose
The Pivot acts as a hub between all the other roles (or rooms).

Perhaps most of all, we need leaders who can maintain the awareness and the balance across all of the Five Element phases and cycles, and cycles-within-cycles, again at every possible scale. Leaders do all of this by focussing on people, and as people, not as 'Human Resources' or worse.

True, some managers do act as leaders, but it's not in the job description as such. And what leadership they do tends to be in their comfort-zone of the thinking-oriented phases of **Preparation** and **Performance**, not so much in the real-time action of **Process**, let alone the, people-centred, feeling-focused work of the **Purpose** or **People** phases.

They won't do much of the leadership between phases, either, not least because that would usually mean treading on some other manager's toes at one or other end of the 'between'.

And in part it's often also because they wouldn't get any credit for doing it, because it is in the largely-undocumentable, largely-untraceable *'between'*-space, where ordinary performance-metrics by definition make no sense.

Another relevant point for this is that management is what business-schools teach. With very few exceptions, they don't teach leadership, at least, not in the sense that has such meaning here. In part that is because most of the manager's tasks can be learnt in the classroom, or via an online training-course. But leadership? No, the only way to learn leadership is on the job, the hard way, year after year, until we know how to instil the trust and commitment in those we lead, including ourselves.

In many cases, managers seem to aim for stasis, to work against change, to remove all uncertainty wherever possible.

By contrast, leaders must work with change. That's the whole point about the activity, after all, that it's always about change, if only in the sense of leading from one activity to the next.

In a Taylorist world, what we need most are managers, whereas leaders, by definition, represent uncertainty, a risk, a threat.

Yet in a post-Taylorist world, where disruptive change is pretty much the *'New Normal'*, what we need most are leaders, real leaders, that is, not mislabelled managers.

Without real leaders, managers tend naturally to sort themselves into rigid hierarchies, each defending their own area, their own share of resources to manage. That works well enough when the business-world is stable, changing only in the routine reshuffles of *'restructuring'.*

But when the world turns unstable, the managers' hierarchies become a principal brake on the flexibility that we need in order to navigate change. And the managers' skill with managing resources may well become non-existent, compared to the abilities of a skilled leader able to obtain needed resources from just about anywhere, seemingly by magic at times.

What organisations need most are real leaders.

24: Who are your anti-clients?

If you are in any kind of business, you will know who your clients are: you deal with them every day. And serving their needs will no doubt take up much of your attention, too. And you, or someone in your organisation, will know who your prospects are, the people who are not clients yet, but who could or should be at some time in the future. Finding them, relating with them and paying attention to their present and future needs will take up a lot of someone's time and attention, even if it's not your own.

But do you know who your *anti-clients*[1] are? Are you even aware that they exist, or how much impact they can have on your enterprise? Because if you don't, and you don't pay attention to their needs too, you could well find yourself out of business… To make sense of who or what those *'anti-clients'* are, and why they are so important, you may need to think differently for a while, perhaps taking in a more expanded view of *'the market'* and a broader-than-usual understanding of *'enterprise'*.

The enterprise and the market

The quick summary is that every market is the intersection of at least three very different *'economies'*: transactions, attention and trust.
(The trust-economy is also known as the reputation-economy, because reputation is a form of second-hand trust that we obtain from others.)
For much of the past century, most organisations focussed almost exclusively on transactions, sometimes barely even recognising the existence of the other economies. Or else assuming that they didn't matter, because large organisations could monopolise attention through mass-media, and ignore customers' concerns by sheer dominance in the marketplace.

But now, access to the internet and mobile-media has changed the game completely. The old days of control and the one-way one-to-many broadcast have gone: welcome instead to a new age of business transparency.
So that means that the attention-economy and trust-economy come right to the front, as almost the only choice you have in this. Meaning that you now must pay real attention to your anti-clients. The other key to this is to recognise that the enterprise is always greater than the organisation. Once we understand this, it becomes useful to categorise the people beyond our organisation in five different ways:
• *clients*
• *prospects*
• *ex-clients*
• *non-clients*
• *anti-clients*

---

1. Anti-clients
For an airport anti-clients could be all those who are opposed to an airport in some way, such as local residents or disgruntled passengers.

Clients and prospects are straightforward: they are people who have done business with you, and who probably will do so in the future.
Every business knows how to work with them, or it wouldn't be in business. They matter a lot, of course, but we can skip over them for now.

Ex-clients are people who've been clients at some point in the past but who, for a wide variety of reasons, no longer engage in transactions with the business. Non-clients are people who have never done business with the business, and are never likely to do so. They are not prospects, and they are not clients, so in terms of the transaction-economy alone, of no apparent value to the business. So many businesses either ignore them, or else try to demand their attention via mass-marketing. Which is dangerous, because either way it's a quick way to convert ex-clients and non-clients into anti-clients.

Anti-clients are people who are the active opposite of clients. Your ex-clients and non-clients are merely not-interested: they will reject your organisation, but only in the form of a passive non-engagement. But anti-clients are different: not only will they not engage in transactions with you, they will actively reject engagement with your and your organisation, and incite others to do the same. In some cases, such as environmental activists, for example, you may have no direct contact with them at all. Even if you are not aware of them, they can still destroy your reputation before you know what's happened. And if you lose your reputation, you have lost people's trust, their attention, their transactions, and any possibility of profit. Without trust, your prospects disappear, your clients become ex-clients, and unless you're aware of your anti-clients, you will have no idea why.

But the worst part of this is that we convert ordinary people into our anti-clients, through our own actions or inactions. For example, many marketers think that using call-centres and the like is just a numbers-game, which it is, but not in the way that they might expect. Call-centres might make profit if just one cold-call in a hundred converts into a real transaction; with online spammers it can be as low as one in a million. But what they do in the process is annoy a vast number of people who are not interested at all and don't like having their attention stolen by the spammers, which can turn them into active anti-clients.

What to do about anti-clients
Step 1: Recognise that anti-clients will always exist, and that they can cause very serious problems for your organisation.

Step 2: Recognise that your anti-clients are never going to be under your control. This is where distinguishing between *'organisation'* and *'enterprise'* is helpful: an organisation is bounded by rules, and you can control within those bounds. But an enterprise is bounded by shared-commitment, where control doesn't work, but honest negotiation can.

Step 3: Recognise that your anti-clients' complaints are real to them, and that is all that matters in practice.
Whether or not those complaints seem real or fair to you is almost irrelevant, and arguing about it is not going to work.

Step 4: Recognise equally that *'giving in'* to every complaint is not going to work for you. Or, ultimately, for the anti-clients either, but they may be too angry to understand that at first. You need to establish common ground where negotiation can take place, preferably before it gets to the level of active anti-client action.

Step 5: Establish the common-ground by identifying the *'vision'* and values that provide the common-cause for every player in the extended-enterprise. These define what quality means within the enterprise, and therefore within your own organisation too.

Step 6: Compare and review the organisation and its procedures against those values and the vision, starting with any customer-facing activities, but eventually extending throughout every aspect of the organisation. This needs to be understood as a quality-review in the most fundamental sense: any improvements here will improve quality within the whole organisation and in its relationships with the broader enterprise, which should reduce the risk of creating anti-clients through carelessness.

Step 7: Use the vision and values as a rallying-point to connect with all of the organisation's stakeholders on their terms, via the various ways in which they they themselves engage with the same vision. In general, this will not and should not be linked directly to the organisation's marketing.

Step 8: Maintain an active watch on social-media, and wherever practicable engage respectfully with all actual or potential anti-clients. One of the most useful tactics to help you in this is to view your anti-clients as allies who can assist in keeping you *'on track'* towards the *'vision'* of the enterprise.
Repeat indefinitely.
Doing this will not only help to pre-empt any potential anti-client problems, long before they cause serious damage, but will also improve your overall quality, and your bottom-line as well.

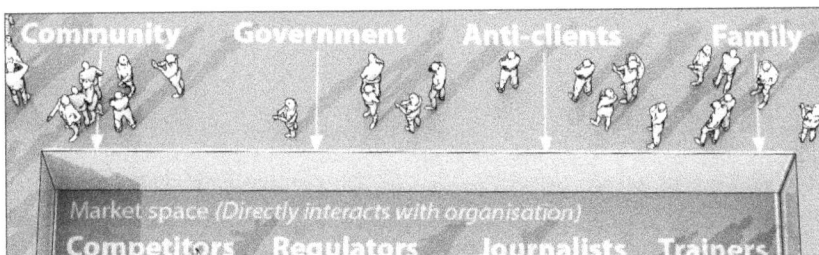

Who are your organisation's anti-clients?

⬠⬠⬠⬠⬠ *Taken from the chapter:* **Who are your anti-clients?**

25: How to write IT standards

Sometimes when IT standards are written the focus can be on streamlining the IT, while unintentionally forgetting the context that IT is meant to be serving. Here we look at some common pitfalls and what can be done to avoid them, using an IT standards document for healthcare, as an example.

Key points

- *anything related to healthcare needs to be centred around the person, the patient, client, family, practitioner, rather than, an IT-system*
- *the enterprise of healthcare is complex, compared to other contexts such as insurance, finance or tax*
- *the enterprise of healthcare is 'political'. Not least because of the competing needs of the patients, clinicians and the business-managers*

Recommendation: 01

Standards should emphasise and address each of those points above. The standard should be easy for IT practitioners to implement, but not ignoring the complexity of healthcare or politics. The patient must come before anything, or any standard will deliver little value and could be dangerously misleading.

Points to avoid

- *prioritisation of business-drivers over healthcare-drivers*
- *no discussion of key healthcare-concerns such as privacy, confidentiality, and security*
- *no discussion of healthcare-time-scales*
- *no discussion of the dynamics of healthcare and healthcare-technology*
- *no discussion of decommissioning*

Decommissioning is often not considered. In IT systems-management, physical decommissioning is often dismissed as *'Somebody else's problem'.* But in a healthcare context, this can't happen, even for IT-systems there can be huge issues around biohazard and data-lifetimes.

Recommendation: 02

Include decommissioning and suchlike as key concerns in the standards.

Recommendation: 03

Ensure that healthcare and the human aspects of health are given priority over the *'business'* of healthcare.

Key values-concerns such as security, privacy, confidentiality and trust should be included in the standards. Since these concerns are central to most patients' lives, as well as core aspects of medical-ethics which should also be at the core of such a document.

Even if the standards relate primarily to IT concerns, the values-concerns for the context for that IT **must** be given a higher priority, as they form part of the reason that the enterprise exists in the first place.

Recommendation: 04
Enterprise wide values-concerns such as privacy, confidentiality and human aspects of security should be priorities in the document.
The drivers and processes to support those concerns should be included in the standards.

There should be references to healthcare time-scales, including their impacts and implications. Healthcare time-scales relate to at least an entire human lifetime, and often far beyond *(such as for epidemiology and similar larger-scale research)*. By contrast, IT-system lifetimes are usually far less than this: a human lifespan averages around 80 years, whereas IT-standards rarely last 40 years[1], databases 20 years, and physical IT-hardware often as little as 3 years.

Even if the standard is focused on IT, data-migration and lifetime-management need to be acknowledged as central concerns for healthcare. This is another reason why decommissioning as a distinct domain in the standard needs to be a high priority.

The dynamics of healthcare and healthcare-technology
Personal consumer-market sensor-technologies, online advisory-services, AI, are all increasing the danger of fragmentation of healthcare/wellness information. They also increase the risks for many forms of damage to patients, families, clients, suppliers, businesses and others.

Recommendation: 06
These issues should be included in the standards: interoperability[2], migration[3] and end-of-unit/technology-life escrow[4]. As well there should be mandatory governance for all of these. For example a technology should not be used in the healthcare field if it doesn't meet these requirements.

The organisation is not the enterprise
If we blur them together, or treat them as the same, we end up with a concept of organisation-as-enterprise in which the organisation has no

---

1. Lifetimes
These numbers are typical example.
2. Interoperability
For example a phone connecting to a smart TV.
3. Migration
For example moving data from one computer system to another.
4. Technology-life escrow.
In brief, a legal agreement to protect users of the software. In case the software provider goes out of business, for example.

purpose other than itself, and no means to connect with or make sense of anything beyond itself. A detailed description of the shared enterprise is shown throughout this book and **Whole Enterprise Architecture**.

Recommendation: 07
Distinguish between 'organisation' and 'enterprise', the 'enterprise' in this case being the broader human-enterprise of healthcare, in all of its many forms. We should be able to describe the healthcare-context beyond the organisation, and make sure the standards are not too generic.

Recommendation: 08
Emphasise the connection to healthcare and the shared enterprise. The shared-story of the enterprise, in this case, the enterprise of healthcare as a whole, including all of its stakeholders. This is what provides shared-purpose between the organisation and the aspects of the shared-enterprise, and provides the actors with the reason to connect, interact and transact through the organisation's services. Without the story, there is no enterprise, just actions upon actions, without any purpose other than in 'what it does'. Without purpose, there's no reason for interactions, for transactions. And without interfaces, there's no means to interact, to transact.

Recommendation: 09
Ensure the standards actually reflect what people do, for example in the healthcare field.

Recommendation:10
Review and revise the standards to ensure that they include explicit processes to minimise and mitigate the risks of IT-related failures, and to learn from and not repeat such failures in future projects.

Recommendation: 11
Ensure that creation, maintenance and monitoring of trust, between all stakeholders, is placed as a central theme for the standards, because without it, the project **will** fail.

Recommendation: 12
Test the standards in real world conditions. Do they work for people who are completely unfamiliar with your standards? Have you explored what happens if the IT system you are designing was to become swamped? What are unlikely but still possible outcomes? Don't just design for best case scenarios. Design for adaptability, assume something unexpected will happen, can your standards cope with rapid and unexpected change? Have you considered the political and legal aspects?

26: Workplace bullying

When power in the workplace changes into bullying, we have a problem.

Probably the most-acknowledged form of *'power'* is that of hierarchical authority, the reporting-relationship between *'boss'* and *'worker'.* The boss gives the orders, the worker must obey, or should do.

There's always potential for conflict in that type of mutually dependent relationship, but, hierarchical power is not in itself the only source of the problem: Power alone does not corrupt.

Power is not the problem. In simple physics terms, power is the ability to do work, and *'doing work'* is what we want to happen in business! The real problem is more subtle, and comes from a single, very human yet highly addictive mistaken view: the belief that we can *'export'* our own inner doubts and discomforts onto others. So, leading to the belief that power is the ability to avoid work…

In human terms *'work'* has a very broad range of meanings. Digging a ditch is work; but so is solving technical problem, managing a team, keeping calm amidst the chaos, and so on. One simple way to understand all these different meanings is to categorise them in terms of *'four dimensions'*:
• *physical work*
• *mental work*
• *relational work*
• *aspirational work*

Aspirational work is perhaps more difficult to recognise as *'work',* but it's about creating a personal sense of meaning and purpose, a sense of self and of relationship with *'that which is greater than self'.* In business we see this expressed as morale, commitment, innovation, creativity and so on. And also as connection to the enterprise via brand or reputation. It takes a lot of work to build a brand, trust, reputation; but it can be destroyed through a single moment's carelessness, and vigilance against that kind of carelessness takes a lot of work too. All of these are work, so in business we need the power to do that work.

Yet all work is hard at times, so it will often seem easier to dump that work onto someone else. This includes relational and aspirational work, in other words, the difficulties of dealing with other people, and of dealing with ourselves. This can lead to many attempts and opportunities to *'export'* that work to others, dumping on others in ways that prevent them from dumping it back. But it can not succeed, because by definition it is our own work. The impossible demand creates frustration, anger, which in turn feeds resentment, and so on. And since the direct path to return the work to where it belongs has been blocked by the *'export',* the only apparent option is to *'counter-export'* via another path, such as put-downs, or the classic slave's tactic of *'work to rule'*[1]. Which also doesn't work because the needed work still does not get done. And spirals ever deeper and deeper towards uncontrollable chaos…

Power is necessary to do the work. The real problem is not power itself, but feelings of powerlessness pretending to be *'power'.*

That is where, and why, reporting-hierarchies can so easily go wrong. Their actual function is one of coordination, to simplify communication (*relational work)*, and decision-making, *(mental and aspirational work)*. But the unbalanced relationship between *'boss'* and *'worker'* also provides a seemingly perfect mechanism for *'export'* of any feelings of powerlessness in the boss. Their position of authority over others seemingly *'entitles'* them to dump on those others in ways where they have no *'right'* of return.

The real problem here is that such dumping will seem to work, for a short while. But since it doesn't actually work, because those feelings of powerlessness are internal to the boss alone, and cannot actually be resolved by anyone else, the same issues will return. All that has happened is that that the boss has in effect manufactured the same feelings of powerlessness in others, which means that the total available *'ability to do work'* has gone down.

In effect it is *'unconstrained incompetence'* versus *'unconstrained competence',* from destructive dysfunctionality to full functionality:
1. *Actively dysfunctional ('power-over'), "prop self up by putting other down" (minimal to no 'ability to do work')*
2. *Passively dysfunctional ('power-under'), "offload responsibility without engagement" (operating within rules only)*
3. *'Best practice' (capable of analysis, some adaptation within rules)*
4. *Relinquish control, "enterprise supports individual difference" (permits adaptation within guidelines, heuristics[2])*
5. *Relinquish command, "individual committed to enterprise", "wholeness-responsibility"(permits principle-based adaptation to uncertainty)*

It all comes down to a single choice in every moment:
• *either everyone wins from what we do;*
• *or everyone loses, including us*

1. Work-to-rule
Work-to-rule is a job action in which employees do no more than the minimum required by the rules of their contract or job and strictly follow time-consuming rules normally not enforced, as a form of protest. Wikipedia

2.Heuristic
A heuristic, is any approach to problem solving that employs a practical method that is not fully perfected, but is sufficient for reaching an immediate, short-term goal. Wikipedia

So despite the common view that *"the only way to win is to make someone else lose"*, there is no *'win/lose'*, it's an illusion. It's actually a form of lose/lose in which a short-term sense of *'winning'* conceals the fact that even the supposed *'winner'* loses from the transaction in the longer term. **In every transaction, the only way that works is when everyone wins.**

This is quite a long way from the usual view of business as *'the drive to beat the competition'* and so on. But that is the challenge: find a way to *'win'* in which everyone wins. Otherwise everyone loses, of which bullying at work is just one of many, many examples…

So what do we do about it?

The key is to tackle the mistaken views: at every opportunity, emphasise and demonstrate that win/lose does not work:
• *propping self up by putting others down does not work*
• *offloading responsibility onto others does not work*
• *the only way that works is when everyone wins*

Incidentally, *'lose/win'*, putting self down to prop other up, or taking on responsibility from others inappropriately, also does not work, for the same reasons. It often seems praiseworthy at the time, but actually feeds the same problems in others, and often in self too. We need to respect the good intentions behind the *'lose/win'*, but we need to challenge it just as much as the more obviously dysfunctional *'win/lose'* behaviours.

Tools such as SEMPER[1] can help in this, providing a mechanism to monitor *'ability to do work'* in many different ways, and identifying appropriate tactics to address each specific type of problem. ' But ultimately it's our responsibility to challenge every source of power-problems, in ourselves perhaps even more than in others. Because if we do not, those power problems such as bullying can destroy the entire enterprise.

1. SEMPER
A brief guide to using SEMPER can be found Tools-for Change-mapping, page 60.

◯◯◯◯◯ Taken from chapter: **Power, responsibility and bullying in the workplace**

27: Ten ways to avoid failure

Success often arises just from avoiding failure. Here are ten strategies for business success:

1. Risk taking
How do you make it safe for people to take risks? How do your people know when risks are appropriate, and when not? What 'safe-fail' fall-back mechanisms could you use to enable people to take safer risks?

2. Flexibility
All those rules and regulations may seem to give little room for manoeuvre, but there are always some options for choice, for chance, for innovation: what are they? How can you use those chances to enhance your organisation's ability to adapt to changing business contexts and conditions?

3. Avoid isolation
Avoid having management hidden away in a bunker, with no-one talking to anyone else. What do you do to ensure you know what is going on, both inside and outside the organisation?

4. Accept you can be wrong sometimes
Allow for the possibility that you may be wrong.

5. Have clear business principles
Corporate social responsibility is an essential survival strategy, especially in the longer term. We need to be clear about our own business-principles, and stick to them.

6. Take time to think
In present-day business, the pressure's always on, always pushing us to do more with less. One of the first things to get sacrificed when it all gets too much is time to think, time to reflect. But if we don't take the time to think about what we're doing, and why, we are likely to find ourselves running into a dead-end. Simple techniques such as the After-Action Review can make a huge difference. By what means can you help shift the mindset from "We don't have time to do this!" to "We don't have time to not do this!"?

7. Do not put too much faith in outside experts
Consultants and contractors do have their roles, but the most important sources of information are usually within the business itself, especially those close to the everyday action. What can you do to to build the right balance between 'outside' and 'inside'? What do you do to create an innovation culture within the business?

8. Love your bureaucracy, but not too much
Bureaucracies do have a real business function, providing 'normal' paths for business communication, to guide, monitor and manage. But whenever we

try to use them as a means of control in business, they grow and grow, limiting communication and creativity. Direction is real, but control is a myth: it doesn't exist. So monitor the monitors, cut away all those meaningless measures, kill off pointless reports that no-one reads: rein in that bureaucracy, and never let it grow without a clear, 'on-purpose' business reason.

9. Don't send mixed messages
Social networks and increased scrutiny mean that mixed-messages will not only be spotted, but can have serious impacts on risk and reputation. One of the best ways to keep consistent on message is to be clear about the links between vision, role, mission and goal, and to have a clear and meaningful business-vision in the first place.

10. Don't fear the future
Formal futures techniques such as business scenarios[1], environmental scanning[2] and causal layered analysis will help to ease those fears. And guide your organisation within what will always be an uncertain future.

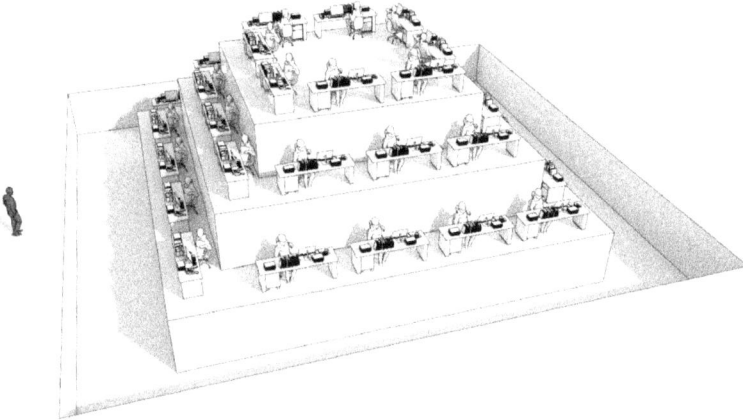

Love your bureaucracy, but not too much...

1. Business scenario
In brief, a method for viewing a business problem from various perspectives.

2. Environmental scanning
In brief, it is used in business to explore how events connect with a business internally and externally.

Part 3:

Business-generalist

This section of the book is an abridged version of
Business-generalist and business-anarchist
www.leanpub.com/tp-eageneralist

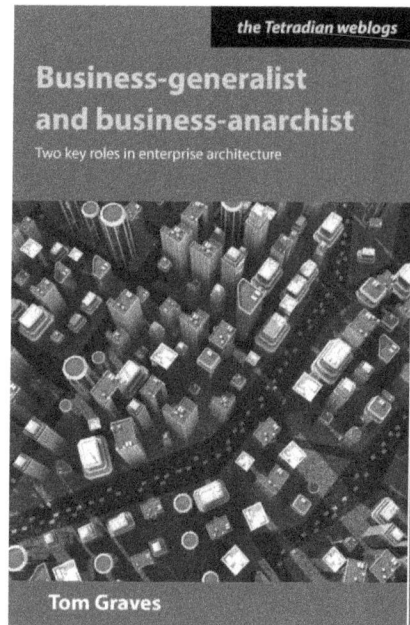

28: How to collect information

What I would like to do here is ignore all of the existing Business-architecture tool-sets, and go right the way back to first-principles:
• *What is the actual aim and value for a tool-set in business-architecture?*
• *What is the actual range of information we need to work with?*
• *How would we collect that information, find our way around that information, connect across that information, share what we find within that information?*

The first two questions are fairly straightforward. Yet what we most need right now, though, is something that will help us deal with the messiness of most real-world business-architecture development. And perhaps the whole point is that we don't know what the information will be, all we know is that it could be just about anything.

We start with a model-type and collect information for that. We then build a diagram. With standard diagram software that is all you're going to get: a diagram, unconnected to any other diagram. With a Business-architecture tool-set, you should also get some kind of store of information, that allows you to shift perspective from diagram-level to object-level, so that you can re-use objects in other diagrams in the same set. Then apply that re-use so as to connect diagrams together as well, preferably even diagrams of different types.

Yet that is so much the usual approach, in fact often the only one built into most of the tool-sets, that it is often difficult to see the hidden assumptions that underlie it. In particular:
• *everything we need is describable in predefined views from predefined viewpoints*
• *every object and relationship we might need is describable in predefined metamodels[1] (This is true even if the metamodel is editable, because it requires definitions for objects and relationships to be in the metamodel before those items can be created and described)*
• *in most cases, object and relationship can be created only in predefined phrases, the relationships are typically expressed with a strict true/false approach with no allowance for necessary inefficiency or fuzziness*
• *in most cases, the model-type allows only one type of visual representation for each type of object or relationship permitted within that model-type*

This approach can work well for final-diagrams to be passed on to solution-architecture, system-design and system-implementation, where they do need things to be as stable as possible. But for the kind of work we do at the level of business-architecture, where the whole point

---

1. Metamodel
A metamodel is a template for building models. For building models that can be compared with each other.

is that everything starts out blurry, messy and uncertain, those are really serious constraints. So serious, in fact, that they make it all but impossible to use those tools to do that part of our work. Which happens to be most of our work...

So let's step right back, and turn each one of those assumptions on its head:
• *we have no idea, at the start, what views and viewpoints we will need.*
  (All we know is that, eventually, we may or will need to identify, create and use
    almost any kind of view or viewpoint)
• *we have no idea, at the start, of what objects or relationships we will need,*
  or the characteristics for either. (Although we know that we are likely to want
    to attach some of them to some kind of predefined meta-model at a later
    stage in development)
• *we have no idea, at the start, of what kind of sentences, structures or*
  business-rules might be needed for objects and relationships. (Although we
  know we are likely to need almost any variety of them at any stage, in line with
  almost any kind of logical approach)
• *we have no idea, at the start, of how best to describe or display*
  any object or relationship. (But we do know that, in many cases, we are going
  to need to be able to show it in different ways for different contexts and
  different stakeholders)

So, inside a Business-architecture tool-set that actually works with the way that we do, we need to be able to handle any type of information, format, connection, display-format, which can change in any way. And still work with them, and link them all together, in a disciplined way.

Where I started with all of this was what I might term the *Burnett Query*, after a former colleague of mine, *Graeme Burnett*, from when we were working together a dozen years or so ago on an information-system for test and inspection in aircraft-research. He said that, for any object, we needed to be able to ask two key questions:
• *tell me about yourself*
• *tell me what you are associated with*

This led us to develop a kind of *'any-to-any'* database-structure, which worked well for that specific requirement. These days, though, I would extend the *Burnett Query* further, to ask, for any object:
• *tell me about yourself, and why you are the way that you are*
• *tell me what you're associated with, and why*
• *tell me how you change, and why*

As relationships are also objects, the last question also handles approaches, the nature of the *'probability, possibility and necessity'* that underlies its approach.

A structure that supports something a lot less like a predefined set of flat diagram-like views, and rather more like a hologram[1] that can be viewed in different ways from any angle:

We perhaps should not take the hologram metaphor too far, but there is another key attribute that we want here:
- *if we cut up a* ❶ *photograph into small pieces, each piece describes a tiny part of the whole, in full detail, but with no self-evident connection to any other part of the whole, or the whole itself*
- *if we cut up a* ❷ *hologram into small pieces, each piece still describes the whole, though in less detail, and still with the connections across the whole essentially intact*

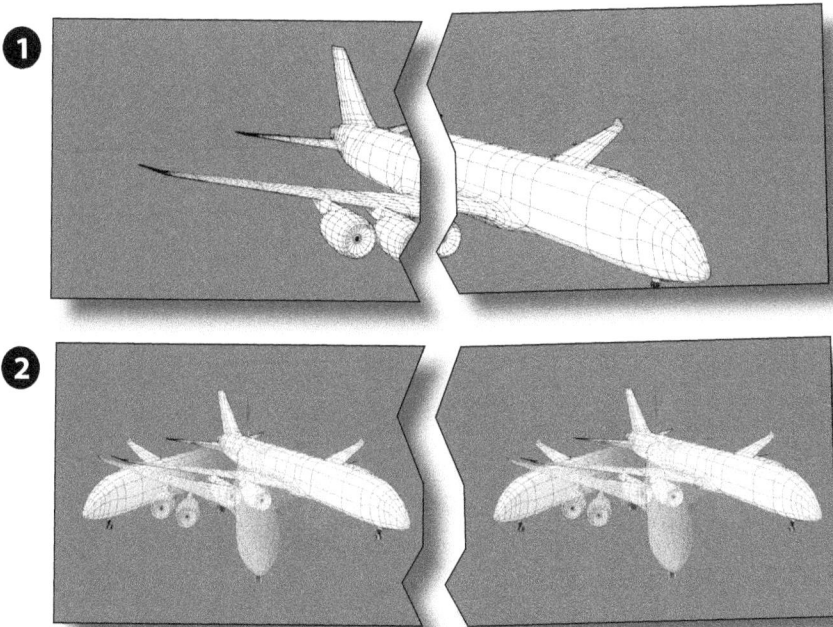

Photographs and holograms differ in how they portray objects

What we really need is somewhere between those two extremes:
- *we need each view into the space to be like a photograph, in full detail for all the elements that we need, hiding everything else that we don't need in that view. (Yet in the background still retain all the dynamic interconnections to every other element)*
- *each piece of information-capture work enables that new information to be interconnected with anything else, as appropriate. (Allowing even the smallest piece of work to add to the available detail throughout the whole)*

Once we get that balance right, though, it gives us incredible power. Almost literally a self-extending hologram, containing and/or referencing all information about that overall context. A large multi-screen system would have access to all of that power, and all of that information. And we would pull out and re-merge extracts to go down onto progressively more constrained systems. Completely consistent, all the way across the entire tool-set-ecosystem. Yet also with any number of different tool-sets and tool-types working in their different ways and with different capabilities and user-experiences, likewise working on the same underlying repository. That's the aim here.

We don't expect that all of it can be done in one tool-set, let alone any one model-type, that is too much to ask, too unwieldy and unrealistic. But it can be done via any suite of tool-sets all connecting to the same underlying data-structure as long as that data-structure provides the right kind of continuity at a low-enough level. The common-factor is not the tool-set, it is the underlying repository. And the repository and its related interchange-format is for any information. This is why it needs to connect at a low-enough level. But once we do have that kind of *'inter-anything'* connectivity, we can do almost anything with it. That is the key; that is the difference.

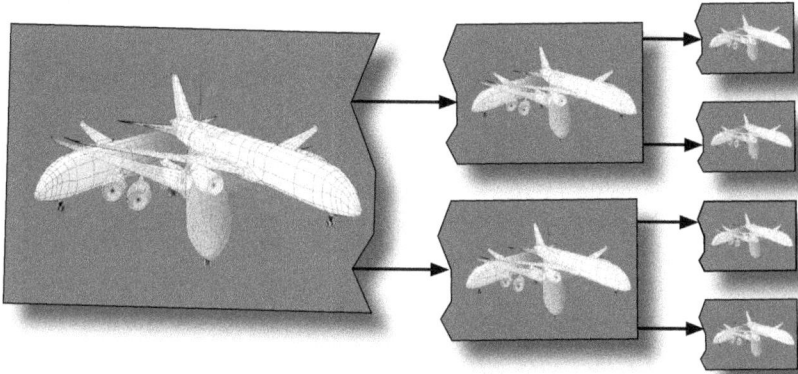

A Business-architecture tool-set that can view the whole context at any scale.

29: Investors

Here we explore some key distinctions between at least five different types
of financial-investors, each with their own fundamentally different
motivations for investment:
• *symbiote (primary-investor), committed to the aims of the enterprise*
• *parasite (beneficiary-investor), interested mainly in returns to themselves*
• *grazer (market-investor), invests in the market, not the organisation*
• *predator (attack-investor), invests for the purpose of gains from destruction*
• *scavenger (derivative-investor), invests solely to 'game' disruption*
  within the market

The Symbiote

This is the only type of financial-investor who is committed to the enterprise
itself. As a true risk-sharing investor, the support will usually be maintained
'though thick and thin' through good-times and bad-times, and usually over
the longer term. The financial investment is primarily to support the aims
of the enterprise: there is a probable desire for financial returns, but that is
often secondary to the focus on support.

The Parasite

The parasite is similar in some ways to the symbiote, but the emphasis is
more on what can be obtained from the organisation, rather than on what
the enterprise itself might need.

The Grazer

This is another form of parasite, but one stage further removed: it has
little to no interest in the underlying enterprise of the organisation, and
its interest in the organisation is only in terms of what of value can be
consumed from it in the short term, after which the grazer will move on.

The Predator

The predator takes this a step further, using some form of financial
investment to take control of the ownership of an organisation,
 and then tear it apart solely for personal gain, through often
illegal activities such as asset-stripping. The enterprise of the organisation,
or its viability beyond the immediate moment, are of no interest whatsoever
to the predator.

The Scavenger

The scavenger is a secondary predator that applies very little investment
of its own, but relies on predators and other *'market forces'* to provide it
with sources for financial-returns. Scavenger-investors thrive on disruption
and instability, typically seeking to create it via leverage of at a-distance
mechanisms such as derivatives-markets. As with the active predator, there
is no actual interest in the enterprise of the organisation itself, but, like a
parasite, may have some interest in the organisation's viability, in order to
maintain the *'game'* for as long as possible.

From the perspective of the individual organisation within the shared-enterprise of that market, any type of investor other than a symbiote is likely to be bad news.

And since as enterprise-architects we are employed by and on behalf of the organisation, not the market, then the needs of the organisation must come first. Which means that any structures we develop must prioritise and support the symbiote-investor relationship above all other types of investor. Which leads to a self-evident need for architectures, and in turn, recruitment models. Those that support the needs of the symbiote-investor: resilient, responsive, self-adaptable, able to keep on track to purpose over the longer-term, and with good financial and other returns. And, if possible, predictable enough to keep the parasite-investors happy too.

Yet that is exactly what Taylorism and similar linear-paradigm models do not give us. What they do give us is brittle, non-responsive, slow-to-change purposeless *'machines',* prone to failure-cycles caused by short-term and a built in inability to *'connect the dots'.*

This is not good for anyone in the enterprise, or any of its direct investors. But it is good for the *grazers*, because it does give good results in the short-term, for a short while, anyway. It is good for the *predators*, because it leaves so many organisations much weaker and less able to defend themselves than they would otherwise be. And it is good for the *scavengers*, because the lack of resilience leaves it wide open to the the kinds of disruption on which the scavengers thrive.

The reality is that much of what we have at present, prioritises the needs of the investor-types in the exact opposite order to what our organisations need: scavengers come first, symbiotes come last. Which is not wise from anyone's perspective. In an ecosystem that's that far out of balance, the predators become so *'successful'* that in killing off all of the prey, they kill off themselves as well. The scavengers would last a little while longer, of course, but when there is nothing left, even they will die too. Eventually…

This is what we have now and so it is what we have to design around. In our architectures, we can't do anything about the politics or the law *(other than keep documenting how and why it doesn't work)*. We can't do much about management-structures *(other than keep documenting how and why they don't work, too)*. What we can do, though, is make it clear why and where our architectures need their generalists.

Part 4:

Business-futures

This section of the book is an abridged version of
Other writing: Experiences
www.leanpub.com/tp-wr-experiences

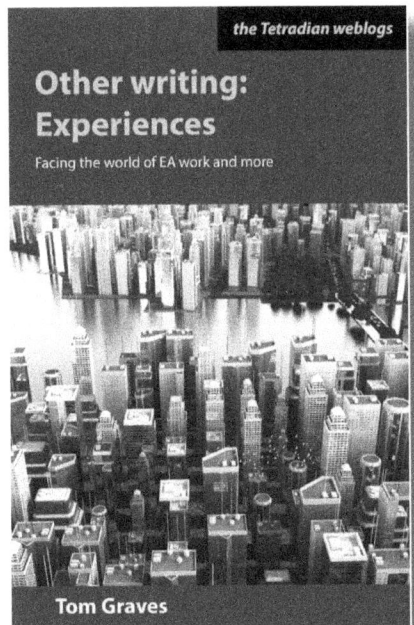

30: Investing in the future

Business tends to focus on the short-term. This next chapter offers a completely different perspective looking at two construction projects with a distinct long-term view...

A few years ago I lived around 60 miles *(100 km)* north of Melbourne, Australia.
While there I planted a large number of trees.

Why?

Well, perhaps the best reason for doing so is in a lovely tale I came across the other day. One of the Oxford *(England)* colleges was having to face the fact that the ancient timbers holding up the roof of their great hall were fast approaching a point beyond which no amount of conservation-work would hold them together: they would have to be replaced. But they were more than **four hundred years** old: where on earth, literally, would they be able to find any equivalent trees for the timber they would need?
After much worry, the conservators finally got round to asking the college's own head-forester for advice. *"Ah, we'd wondered when you'd be coming round here for those"*, he said. *"When our foresters from the old Elizabeth's time cut down the oaks for those beams of yours, they planted their replacements too. They've been maturing nicely over the past century or two: I'd say they're about the right size for you now. When did you say you'll need them, ready for the builders to use? We'll have them ready for you by then."* And before the conservators could get over their shock and relief, the forester quietly added, *"We'll plant their replacements at the same time, of course."*

Yet there's also a deeper *'why'* beyond the merely pragmatic. I was reminded of this again today whilst re-reading an old favourite, the book-version of *Jean Giono's* short-story *The Man Who Planted Trees*.
Planting trees, both literal and metaphoric, creates the possibilities for a better future, for everyone. And yes, that was one of the real inspirations for all of that effort of mine, so far away now in both time and space.

For quite a while, several years, I literally planted trees, all round the block and house where I used to live. It was almost completely bare when I moved there. I planted some three thousand trees and shrubs in all: all done by hand, all watered by hand every day at first, day after day after day, in one of the worst droughts there so far this century.
It was pretty heartbreaking when the kangaroos smashed the tree-guards down and the rabbits ate the rest; it was pretty heartbreaking, too, to discover the hard way that an entire planting of one species of tree, billed as frost-resistant, wasn't. And it didn't help when some young idiot in a stolen car overshot the junction at the top of the road, ploughing through two layers of fencing and three lines of young trees before the car came to a halt and he ran away, with the engine still running…

There's a very good reason why this kind of thing is known as *'a labour of love'*: it's a long, hard slog, with serious expense in money and time and effort, and with nothing much to show for it for a long long time. Most of the real growth didn't start happening until the rains came back, almost a decade after I had started. Yet despite all of those hardships and traumas, the trees are at last getting somewhere.

But here's the twist: I don't get any supposed *'benefit'* from having done all of that work. Not now, anyway. I sold the place more than seven years ago: and those trees didn't even register as the smallest blip on the *'valuation'* of the property, of course. Someone else now has all of the benefit from everything that I did back then.

The fact is that people who plant trees rarely do see much direct benefit from all of their hard work. And it doesn't matter. Or actually, it does: it matters that the work was done, otherwise those trees would not be there now, providing all of those many services that trees do.

People who see only the *'now'* want everything now. That's pretty much a description of our entire so-called *'economy'*, in fact. Yet not everything happens all at once: some things do take time to come to fruition, whether we like it or not. And in many cases, yes, the time-to-fruition really is measured not in days, but in decades, or more.

Many people, it seems, look only to the harvest right now, and don't think of what has to happen before that harvest can exist.

In the meantime, some people do think about what will be needed to make that future happen, and take action in the now, to make the future possible at that future time. *(And that work, somehow, has to be paid for in 'the now', too… otherwise that future won't happen…)*

Futurists are foresters: they plant trees, and nurture them.
Sometimes those *'trees'* may be a bit more metaphorical, planting ideas, tools, ways of thinking, but trees nonetheless: trees that take time to grow, many years of quiet, tender, often-unrewarding, often-heartbreaking care, so as to be ripe and ready for the harvest when their time comes.

The best time to plant a tree is twenty years ago.

If we can't do that, go back in time to do that, then the next-best time is now.

Planting trees of all kinds, metaphoric and literal, for a better future, for everyone.

⬠⬠⬠⬠⬠ *Taken from the chapter:* **Planting trees**

www.ingramcontent.com/pod-product-compliance
Lightning Source LLC
Chambersburg PA
CBHW040758220326
41597CB00029BB/4986